A GUIDE

FOR

HUNTING

GHOSTS

Alison Smith

DEDICATION

This book is dedicated to my husband Jason, my parents, Scott and Nancy and my brother, Austin. Without the love and support of the most important people in my life, I'd never have been able to become a Ghost Hunter. From Jason buying me my first few pieces of equipment to my dad introducing me to the collective works of Hans Holzer, each of you has played a role in helping me get started and I'm forever grateful. I love you all and I am thankful for you every day.

CONTENTS

ACKNOWLEDGMENTS

HERE'S TO THE NIGHTS THAT TURNED INTO MORNINGS WITH THE FRIENDS THAT TURNED INTO FAMILY

- UNKNOWN

First I want to thank my PRONE family who have been through all these life lessons with me and encouraged me to write this book. To Rob, my brother! Thank you for ALL your help, this book would still be a word doc on my laptop without you. To Cheryl, my sister, my sitting on rocking chairs, living forever friend. Thank you for always being there no matter what craziness is going on and for casting such magic in my life ;) To Kathy, I know you share the same love for PRONE that I do, it wouldn't be the same without you. To Andy, you are just fine the way you are, I would never change a single thing about you, now stop apologizing! To Steve, thank you for being my rock, psychic or not! To Jeff, how you ended up in the crazy world of PRONE has to be fate, you probably could have found a way more normal group to join…but I'm glad you didn't. To Mike, we loved you, and then missed you and we are so glad you missed us too. Each of you makes this group what it is and I can't explain how proud I am of PRONE, of where we came from and where we are now.

I also want to thank all the people who have let us investigate and especially those who have also become our friends. We love you all, thanks for sharing your ghosts with us!

INTRODUCTION

Like most people who "ghost hunt", I've been fascinated with all things paranormal since I was a kid. It wasn't until all of the TV shows started coming out when I realized it was a real thing I could actually do. I think this is a situation a lot of people find themselves in now. After doing a little digging, I was shocked to find out not only how many allegedly haunted locations there were in my area, but how many local paranormal groups there were. At that point I would have found it surprising if there was just one, but there were literally dozens.

It was very difficult to see where to start. I didn't personally know anyone involved in the field yet and couldn't seem to convince anyone else I did know to try and get their foot in the door with me (that's certainly changed now though!). I finally found an "in" through a local meet-up online.

1

These are public events open to anyone with common interests. There happened to be a paranormal one being held out of the Iron Island Museum in Buffalo, NY. I joined the site and started going to these public meetings. The great thing about it was the fact that there was also a mini-investigation after every meeting since it was held in a haunted building.

The meet-up was an interesting way to step into the paranormal world. Being open to the public, it attracted people from several established groups, freelancers (these are people who may not be committed to a single group, but may tag along with several, do their own thing, and have plenty of experience investigating that way), and people like me who had no experience, but were very curious about the whole thing. Being a skeptic (and admittedly maybe even a little cynical back then), I approached all of this very cautiously.

During the meetings, I remained quiet because that's just how I am and I didn't think I could just cut in being so new to all of this. It was amazing to see how many people had such differing opinions on everything though. Everyone had different ways of doing things and it was obvious right from the start that not everything is exactly like you see it on TV.

When the investigations would start, I ended up tagging along with a number of different groups and freelancers. While I was impressed with the activity most nights, I didn't really think I fit in with any specific group. I met some nice people that I still know today, but I definitely got the impression from some people that they didn't want me around at all. Joining a group was never my intention when I began though. I was just trying to see for myself if there was anything to this "ghost hunting" business.

I had gone to meetings for several months and was thinking I was just about done. It was fun for what it was, but I thought I had done all that I could do. I bounced around investigating with almost everyone and had gotten to know what to expect out of Iron Island (which for the record impressed me).

During what I was thinking about being my last investigation at least for a while, turned out not to be that at all. I ended up meeting Alison and a few other members of PRONE at the meet-up. Right from the start the difference between her and PRONE and all of the other people I had tagged along with was obvious. They were actually the first ones to really try to involve me on the investigation. Alison wanted to know what I thought about things and what I believed was the proper way of doing things. One of our earlier conversations was about whether or not provoking was a good thing (it isn't). The way that Alison and the rest of the group treated me made sense after hearing they more or less went through the same thing I did trying to start out and only began the group after being ignored or turned away by others.

It's not that every group or person I investigated with before rejected me; it's just that this was the first group that I really seemed to agree with 100%. Later on, Alison contacted me through e-mail to invite me on investigations outside of the meet-up with PRONE and at other locations as well. It was surprising after not having contact outside of the meet-up with anyone else I had met there. I had no idea at the time, but my early investigations with the group were almost like a "trial run" to see if I really was a good fit. I started to love what I was doing then with the role I played; trying to debunk things and work with the equipment. I've been doing it ever since after being asked to join the group four years ago.

It's impossible for a group to accept and welcome in every person that asks, but we can at least point them in the right direction. We still get people at random conventions and presentations asking to join up with us, but not knowing that person at all makes it impossible to say whether or not they would be a fit with the group or if they would even want to be a part of the group when they got to know us. It's very hard to get involved with the paranormal and stick around. I just happened to get lucky.

There are countless books out there that tell you how to ghost hunt, but I don't think I've heard of any that help steer people in the right direction on how to start and deal with all of the other factors involved with the paranormal such as ethics, keeping a group organized, and dealing with the public/clients. I know that Alison has dealt with all of these things for years and still has our group going strong when countless others have come and gone.

~Rob Gallitto
Author of *"Modern Technology and Paranormal Research"*

The Logo of the Paranormal Researchers Of Niagara and Erie

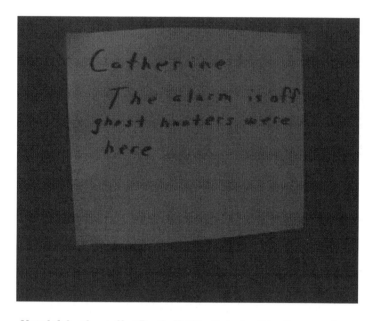

Note left by the staff at Bertie Hall in Ontario, CA after one of our investigations.

1. WHY GHOST HUNTING?

Where it all began....

So you think you want to be a ghost hunter? Let me begin by telling you right up front that it is not what you see on TV. It's not nearly as glamorous and can be quite time consuming. It involves a major personal commitment and lots of time away from friends and family. Usually it doesn't pay and in fact costs more than most hobbies or interests. The purpose for me wanting to write this book is because we have no set rules to go by when it comes to ghost hunting and knowing what to do can be very confusing depending on where your information is coming from.

We have no ethics that are agreed upon across the board. There is much controversy about theories and practices and I wanted to put something together that could act a guide for people who were looking for standards. So if you can look past all of this to see the field for what it is, than let's talk about how to do this in a professional and responsible way. The best place to start is always at the beginning....

From the time that I was little I was always intrigued by unexplainable things likes ghosts. Maybe it was due to growing up with Scooby Doo cartoons on Saturday mornings or reading Goosebumps books, or maybe it came from somewhere else. I grew up hearing stories of my great grandmother's haunted house. My mom, aunts and uncle would often talk about seeing faces in the basement windows while playing outside or watching shadows pass doorways in the middle of the night. One would think that stories like these would inspire fear in a young child, but instead it made me more curious. I didn't grow up in your typical haunted house. We never had any paranormal activity in my house, but I did have experiences throughout my life that led to my current path. I feel like people are meant to do things in their life and I was meant to hunt ghosts.

I had my first paranormal experience when I was about 5 years old. My mom was a home health aide for a woman who had terminal cancer. I had never met this lady, but knew her name, Rose Mary, from hearing my mom talk about her. My mother developed a fondness for her and was very sad when she passed. A few months later, I became ill and my mom had to take me to the local hospital in the middle of the night. I remember sitting in the examination room waiting for the doctor and seeing this lovely lady moping the floor outside the room. She looked up from her work and smiled at me. I turned to my mom and said "Mommy, that lady looks just like Rose Mary". As my mom stood there dumbfounded, because indeed this woman looked just like her, a guard passed by the woman. As he walked passed her he smiled and said "Good night Rose Mary". My mom was shocked and couldn't explain any of this. All she knew was that somehow her daughter had just recognized a woman she had never met.

A few years later, I went on a family vacation to Gettysburg, PA. For a little background, I have always been interested in the Civil War, everything from the clothing to the customs of the time. So much so that during a creative writing time in grade school (just prior to our trip), I decided to write a story about a woman named "Mary" and her role in the war. This in itself may seem strange since most kids were probably writing about their favorite sports team or favorite food, but I think it's safe to assume that I was a little different at this point. My story involved a woman who went out onto the battle fields at Gettysburg and helped to identify the fallen in order to let their families know what had become of their loved ones. She took great care in this and wandered the fields constantly searching.

During a tour of a particular location while on our trip, I started to feel like I'd been in this place before. I seemed to know my way around and was even telling my mom and brother where things were in the house and what they were used for. As I entered one room, I saw a photo of a woman who looked very much like the Mary I had written my story about. I pointed this out to my mom and when my mom looked at the photo, she noted that even though we were in Jenny Wade's House, her real name was not Jenny at all. Her real name was actually Mary Virginia Wade. I couldn't explain how I had described this woman and somehow seemed to know her name.

The last experience I want to share is probably the one that shaped my desire to try to understand what happens when people pass on the most. Lots of people have had similar experiences to this one. As far as making contact goes, this seems to be one of the most common. This is how it unfolded for me.

I was close to my grandfather on my mom's side of the family while growing up. Being the first born grandchild, there was a special bond we had. He had a special nickname for me and I would come over and drink all his ginger ale. I hadn't really lost anyone close to me before his passing and his came quickly with no warning. I went to bed one night in February in 1993, I was just shy of my 13th birthday. I had a dream that night that my grandfather came into my room and sat at the end of my bed. He told me that he had to go away and not to be sad. He seemed calm and happy and I remember waking up and feeling calm. It turns out he passed that morning while on vacation with my grandmother, states away. It was sudden and devastated my family. He was larger than life, but I didn't cry at his wake or his funeral. I felt like I had already said my good byes.

These are a few of my first experiences that I can remember but not the only one I've had. This type of thing has happened to me throughout my life and led me to want to try to understand paranormal activity and the circumstances surrounding it. I have been investigating the paranormal for a number of years now and can't say I'm any closer to getting those answers. If anything I have more questions now than when I started, but this is what keeps me searching.

I had thought about writing a book about ghost hunting and its fundamentals from the start, but didn't think I had gained enough experience to do so until recently. You see, I always say there are no experts in this field, in fact you will hear it repeated throughout this book. We are all students and are learning by trial and error. I have had my own growing pains in this field and wanted to share what I know so it's easier for people coming in. The paranormal field can be a cold dark place and it's hard to know where to turn for information. As I share with you my lessons learned, please keep in mind that this is by no means the only way to do things. I suggest you try things out yourself and tweak them as you see fit. Merely use this as a guide to develop your own methods and don't be afraid of what you might discover, after all the only way to get to the light is through the dark.

Alison Smith

2. HISTORY OF GHOST HUNTING

Where did we come from and where are we going?

In order to understand where the future of ghost hunting is headed, we have to understand our roots. Believe it or not ghost hunting did not start in the mid 1990's. People have been trying to make contact with the other side from the beginning of time. Ancient societies built pyramid type structures that could reach the heavens. They believed in a life after death and had elaborate funeral rituals to ensure that their loved ones had an easy passage through this life and into the next. They buried people with objects they would need when they "woke up" on the other side.

Medicine men and women in cultures all over the world held rituals in the dead of night to contact spirits for help or guidance. Native American cultures believe that their ancestors are still with them and help them on a daily basis. You can see this reoccurring theme of life after death in almost every culture in the world in one form or another. This idea of contacting the dead is by no means a new one.

For our purposes we are going to focus on the early history of ghost hunting as it relates to what we do now. And we will begin with a gentleman by the name of Sir Arthur Conan Doyle and his belief in life after death. Doyle is probably most well-known for his fictional works about a detective named Sherlock Holmes, but his contributions to the paranormal field are what we are going to exam.

Doyle suffered great loss in his life. His wife, son, brother and a few other relatives passed away within a short time span. Due to these losses, Doyle began to seek out proof that there was life after death and what he found was a religious movement called Spiritualism. This movement was based on the idea that contact with spirits who had passed can be made through a medium. This movement still continues today and is practiced in certain townships, such as Lillydale, NY. Doyle was excited by this possibility and began to immerse himself in the paranormal field. He joined a local organization whose sole purpose was to try to prove or disprove if paranormal activity was real.

In 1921, he wrote a book based on the Cottingley Fairy photos. You have most likely come across these photos at some point, but if not you may want to look them up online just for history sake. The most famous photo features a young girl surrounded by dancing fairies. These photos were later debunked, but at the time really did seem quite convincing. For Doyle, these were proof that things existed out there that should be explored.

Doyle truly believed mediums and psychics could contact the dead and did his best to try to convince his colleagues of this. This desire led to a most unlikely friendship between Doyle and a famous magician, Mr. Harry Houdini. Although Houdini had the opposite views of Spiritualism than Doyle did, there was a friendship there until Doyle became convinced that Houdini had supernatural powers of his own. This did not go over well with Houdini and he tried to convince Doyle that what he did was merely magic tricks meant to entertain. The two had a very public falling out as a result.

For our purposes we have to credit Doyle with brining the idea about communicating with the dead into the public eye. A man with his background lent a certain amount of credibility to the Spiritualist movement. He may not have convinced as many people as he wanted to do, but this belief in life after death opened a door and gave him solace that he would be able to be with his family when he passed and that until that time, they were not totally lost to him on this earthly plane.

You may not think Houdini has a place in talking about the history of ghost hunting, but he does. Houdini made it his mission to expose fraud in the Spiritualist community after he felt he was taken advantage of by a medium who supposedly tried to contact his deceased mother. Houdini made it a personal aspiration of his to show the world that there was no such thing as a medium. With his background in magic he was able to expose a lot of the mediums and their tricks. He made his own "spirit photograph" to show how easy it was to hoax. He even went as far to attend séances in disguise. He famously told his wife that when he died he would try to communicate with her if it was possible. He gave her a phrase to use and on every anniversary of his death for 10 years, his wife held a séance to try to make contact. Houdini's wife claimed this contact was never made and gave up trying. Houdini was the first public figure to take a stance against spirit communication. He is the first true "debunker" that we can look to, but he wasn't the only one.

If there ever was a skeptic of the paranormal it would have to be Harry Price. It's important to note that Price was a skeptic but not a cynic. Cynics are people who will never; no matter what the circumstances are, believe in paranormal phenomena. No matter what evidence is presented, they will always find a way to discount it. Price exposed fraud, but he also believed in ghosts. In fact some of the methods he employed on his cases we still use today. Whereas Doyle was a believer, Price was an investigator. He wanted to see for himself and spent most of his life doing just that.

He had a great dislike for people he felt were cheating the public and giving them false hope. He exposed the spirit photographer, William Hope as a fraud along with many others. Price's biggest pet peeve was physical mediumship. His most well-known case of exposure was that of medium Helen Duncan. Duncan was paid a sum of money by an organization Price belonged to in exchange for the ability to study her scientifically while she conducted séances. At the end of his investigation, Price concluded that Duncan was merely regurgitating cheese cloth that she had swallowed early and not actually producing the ectoplasm that she claimed. This had become a common trick of fraudulent mediums of the time. Duncan became the first medium to be tried for fraud and false mediumship and Price gave his evidence as part of her trail. She was found guilty based on his conclusions.

In terms of ghost hunting Price is famous for the investigation of Borley Rectory in Essex, England. He wrote two books about the haunting and ran the investigation in a way that was as controlled as it could have been at the time. People claimed to have experienced paranormal activity such as hearing footsteps, seeing the ghost of a nun, hearing bells ringing, seeing lights in windows and even reports of a ghostly horse drawn carriage were made. Price was first brought in by a reporter and experienced the phenomena himself. When the property became vacant he rented it and put out an ad for people to act as observers of the property. He had "observers" watch the place and take notes on any strange phenomena that occurred.

Price had the daughter of an associate make contact with the ghosts using a planchette and a talking board. Two spirits came forth; the first was that of a nun who supposedly was killed on the property for indiscretions and the other was a spirit of a man who claimed he would burn down the rectory and that the bones of a murdered person would be discovered. The rectory did burn down, but not from a ghost. An oil lamp was knocked over and caught fire burning a large portion of the building. The bones were another story.

After the fire, Price returned to dig in the cellar and found two bones that he believed to be from a young woman. People in town thought they were those of a pig, but the mystery remains since the bones were given a proper burial in a local cemetery and never examined further. None of the controversy surrounding the rectory stopped Price from calling it "the most haunted house in England" and forever establishing it as being known for its paranormal activity.

Moving forward into more modern times, we touch on the man who is known to have first coined the term "ghost hunter". Interestingly enough it was Price who first used the term much earlier, but it never stuck. Hans Holzer is considered by many in the field to be the father of modern day ghost hunting. He wrote over 100 books on the paranormal and participated in countless investigations, the most famous being the Amityville Horror case. Holzer believed fully in life after death and in the use of mediums. He thought they had a connection to the other side that he could not make. He used a notebook, a recorder and a pen to document some very interesting cases. Much the same way we do today, Holzer would take notes while the medium went into trance and then would take that information and go back to try to corroborate it through research.

Holzer believed in ghosts, spirits and what he termed "stay behinds". He defined ghosts as energy that was left behind that could be picked up by sensitive people, such as mediums, spirits are similar to what we term "an intelligent haunt", something that can communicate back and forth with us and "stay behinds" were spirits that found themselves stuck in this plane of existence. Perhaps they have unfinished business or had passed tragically, but they cannot for whatever reason, move on.

Because Holzer worked closely with many mediums, he had his fair share of doubters. Skeptics took up every chance to disprove his research by finding flaws in the information received from the mediums. Since trance is not an exact science it made it difficult to prove credibility one way or the other. Just as a person doesn't always tell the truth neither do spirits. They can, just as we do, slant things to be more in their favor especially if they engaged in behavior they are not proud of. Using mediums in investigations is always controversial, but can have big benefits as we will discuss further in this book.

The next best thing to using a medium is being able to contact spirit yourself. That is just the case for our next people to give mention to, Ed and Lorraine Warren. Lorraine and her husband Ed were involved in some of the biggest paranormal cases of our time. They wrote many books and completed countless investigations. But they also bring a new flavor into ghost hunting, the demon. Ed Warren was a self-proclaimed demonologist. It's important to note that there is much controversy about this term to begin with. First off, believing in demons is a Christian ideal so depending on your religious views in general this may not even be something you buy into. I believe that if you were a jerk in this life and you pass away, chances are good you may be a jerk in the afterlife too. So for me, I do believe that there are negative spirits but not like in the commercialized red eyed versions that try to possess humans for their souls. For all the investigations I've been on, I have never met a demon, a jerk once in a while, but not a demon.

Possession was not a new idea in the 1970's and 1980's but with cases like the Amityville Horror and movies like "The Exorcist", possession became the talk of the paranormal field. This culminated with the case of Arne Johnson, in 1981. He killed his landlord and was charged with murder. He pled not guilty by reason of demonic possession. The Warrens claimed he was possessed by a demon and couldn't control his actions. There are some groups that still believe in demons and possession, I'm not going to spend any more time on it, but if you have further interest the Warrens' have written many books about their experiences with demons and the devil himself.

So this takes us to the 1990s and the start of couch ghost hunting. TV shows have become the best outlet to further the paranormal field. Most of the groups in existence today are a direct result of being exposed to the media version of ghost hunting, me included.

The important thing to know is that it should not be your sole information source on how to hunt ghosts because it's made for TV! You owe it to yourself to do some research and learn the history. Even if these ideas and methods seem outdated there are still lessons to be learned. Always remember that there is a place for the skeptics and the believers. We need each other to stay grounded and to move forward in this field. No matter what the future holds, we will do ourselves a true disservice to forget our past.

Alison Smith

Photo of the infamous "Death Tunnel" at Waverly Hills

3. IMPACT OF THE MEDIA

From TV, to movies, radio and magazines, the influence of the media is everywhere…

Without question we live in a technologic age where equipment and the ability to share and experiment are constantly at our fingertips, but is this always a good thing? Like most viewpoints, there are two sides to this argument. First we will examine the good points to our increased media in the paranormal field and then take a look at what can hinder us due to the same ideals.

Sharing of evidence:

Before laptops, Facebook and the internet how did paranormal groups share their evidence? There weren't many outlets but most came from print. You wrote a book or an article and had it published, often only to be seen by a limited few and never to hit mainstream or the masses. This all changed for us with the coming of the digital age. Until the use of digital recorders sharing a simple EVP was difficult and often compromised the original recording due to rerecording the sample in order to share it. Now we think nothing of loading our raw recordings into the computer and emailing clips we have questions about to members of our group for further discussion.

Even the way we present evidence to our clients couldn't be done without the use of a cd burner and a laptop. We now have filters to put the EVPs through, we can amplify noises and voices, cut the total clip to just what we need to hear and even change the frequency.

The ability to change all these things scares me. With technology comes responsibility. In a field with no set standards or codes of conduct, there is nothing to prevent people from altering evidence other than the honor system. Over the years I've heard EVP's that have been altered so much that they now sound digitized. If you take a clip of anyone talking you can manipulate it to sound "demonic" or menacing. Unfortunately with the current state of media exposure, it's clear that investigators feel compelled to present the client with some sort of evidence.

Every TV show seems to wrap up an investigation in a nice 30 minute episode complete with evidence of a haunting. How many times have you watched a show where they came up with nothing at the end of it? Not often of course, otherwise there would be no show to watch. If no evidence was found the viewers would stop tuning in and the shows would cease to exist.

One of my biggest pet peeves with TV shows and their EVP evidence is how they will tell you what they think the clip says before they play it. This automatically puts that idea in your head and influences your perception. If you couldn't make it out the first time you heard it, you now think it says

"I can see you", because that's what came across the screen as they played it. There is a standard way that we handle this type of evidence, but we'll discuss it further later on.

To give credit where it's due, it's also fair to note that most of the investigations you see are actually done over the course of a few days. We all know it's easier to catch evidence based on the amount of time you are there. We also have to consider that they record their episodes at haunted locations. They can pick and choose where they want to go and know what will make for good TV as opposed to taking every lead. We are often chasing down every report to try to find that one that will yield a great piece of evidence or to be able to debunk the supposed phenomena in order to ensure the client is comfortable in their home or business.

Taking photos has become easier also with the use of digital cameras. The photos are much clearer and have less anomalies than the pre -digital models. Also sharing photos has become as simple as sending an email. We can also blow up, zoom in and out and change the colors of them to enhance our evidence. Again this makes me uncomfortable because so much can be manipulated through means available to everyone. If you doubt that this happens, just go to your computer and type in "ghost photos". You will be amazed how many photos come up that have clearly been manipulated but claim to be legitimate.

There are even apps for phones now that are meant to fake out your friends by superimposing images of ghostly figures into your everyday photos. This reminds me of the disposable cameras where ghosts would show up in the photos once they were developed. These can be a lot of fun, but it gives our field less credibility when groups try to pass it off as real evidence. This is why we need to set standards, we have to be able to trust that evidence from another group is just as good and as creditable as are own.

Another aspect of the media we have to acknowledge is the increase in the technology of our equipment. As the number of paranormal shows increase so does the amount of equipment and its capabilities. A person could easily go broke trying to outfit themselves and their group with the equipment out there. My advice is don't do it! Most of that stuff will end up lying around collecting dust, looking cool and never being used.

One of the new trends that I am on board with is combining two or more pieces of equipment. Although the hybrids are more expensive, at least there is a valid idea behind them. It's also interesting to see what other people are making and how it's working out on investigations. My own group has some new and different equipment that was made by our Tech Manager, Rob. Most of those ideas came from something we had seen or heard about through media of some sort.

Along with the inclusion of the digital recorder and the digital camera has been the use of the digital camcorder. Long gone are the days of changing tapes and trying to figure out to get the tapes copied to VHS to be shared by others. The process has again been simplified to downloading the data to your laptop and emailing clips as needed. TV shows have been a big supporter of this kind of evidence since when it's caught it's harder to dispute and usually way more impressive, but it's also the least common captured out of the three.

With the advances in camcorders we can now do something or predecessors could not. We can see in the dark. TV shows would be no fun to watch if you couldn't see the scared looks on the faces of the participants as they heard a noise or saw a shadow. And again between Youtube and Facebook there are no shortages of amazing video clips of ghosts caught on tape, or are there?

We always have to take evidence with a grain of salt, especially when it comes from a source we don't know. But with the addition of night shot and IR lights to most camcorders, this kind of evidence is being seen more and more. A digital camcorder is a great addition to your arsenal for ghost hunting, but it requires caution at the same time. Evidence should always be analyzed as opposed to being taken at face value. Just because you see it on TV or read it on the internet doesn't make it true.

We have to respect the fact that without the increase in media attention to the paranormal field many of us would still be conducting investigations and pursing ghosts in the shadows. Since the TV shows and the attention they have brought, it has become acceptable to ghost hunt in general. People are more comfortable discussing their experiences, inviting investigators in and talking with them about the findings. The paranormal has become more main stream and intriguing as it comes into our living rooms on a regular basis.

But what we have to ask ourselves is why do we want to do it? Are you looking for fame and fortune or do you truly have a desire to answer the questions you have and to help people? Once you figure this out, you'll be ready to move forward. I always knew I wanted to help others and better understand the phenomena itself.

When I was first asked to give a presentation to the public, I enlisted a few core members of my group and we started by researching, not by watching reruns of paranormal shows. If you're looking for the fame and think there is a demon around every corner, put this book down and pick up your remote. You won't find the answers you're looking for here but you may find them on an all day marathon of your favorite ghost hunting show.

4. TO START A GROUP OR TO JOIN ONE

So if you are still reading this, I think we can both assume that you are here for the same reasons I am. And in getting started there is that inevitable question that has to be dealt with first and foremost. Do you start a group or join one already in existence? There are perks to both of these options, but first I want to tell you why I ended up starting a group.

As I stated earlier on, I have always been interested in the paranormal. About 6 years ago my interest turned into something else entirely. I had discovered a particular TV show that was making it acceptable to go out, investigate places and talk about their experiences. Most groups that were formed around this time and for years afterward are based on the model from this particular show, whether they admit it or not, I like to give credit where credit is due. So I set out to find a local group to join.

I started out by sending emails to the groups in my area and got little to no response. I was feeling very discouraged because this was something I really wanted to do. I kept hitting brick wall after brick wall. Groups were either filled or not taking new members, wanted to charge crazy membership fees or just plain out did not respond. I joined a website that focused on the paranormal and started posting inquires about groups or how to get started. People told me to do some research, which I did but this just furthered my desire to get some hands on experience.

Through my postings on this website, I started to communicate with a woman in a town a few over from mine. I was mentioning this website to a few coworkers one day and it turns out the person I was communicating with was also my co-worker! I have this belief that you are where you are supposed to be at any given moment, this has become a reoccurring theme in my life and this was no exception. We started to get together outside of work and talk about ghost hunting and what it meant to us.

We realized we shared a lot of the same beliefs and instead of trying to fit into someone else's ideals, we decided to start our own group. PRONE (Paranormal Researchers of Niagara and Erie) was born in a local bookstore over iced tea on a hot day in August of 2008.

And like most groups we figured if we had a name, a website and a logo, we were in business. I say this tongue in cheek, because it's funny just how naïve we were looking back on this now. Neither one of us had any idea the blood, sweat and tears that would go into running a group. Not to mention the amount of time that would have to be devoted to coordinating, scheduling, documenting and figuring things out, in order to be successful.

But there are some good points in being able to run your own group. The best one is that ultimately you are in charge, you make the rules and the decisions, and there will be a lot of them to make. It's up to you how your group will be perceived and to decide what your ideals will be. Will you charge for membership or investigations? Will you take a scientific approach or a metaphysical one? Will you be a group that provokes or is that something you won't stand for? There are a lot of things to consider when shaping your group, but this will be based on your overall vision.

Being in charge also allows you to set the pace. Are you going to investigate every week or a few times a month? What kinds of investigations will you book? Do you want to concentrate on one type more so than another? How do you feel about traveling? Do you prefer to stay close to home? How many members do you want? Does it matter if they are guys or girls? In the beginning we thought our group would just be made up of women, but that changed as we met more people.

Being flexible is the most important thing to remember when trying to have a successful group. You can't control what others do and you have to be prepared for investigators to cancel, get sick or even leave the group. The longer you are established the more changes you will go through. Although my group has held true to our original vision, a lot has changed over the years. Sometimes it's hard to be in charge and be responsible for so much and you may even become resentful of other members you don't feel are pulling their weight. We will talk about some ways to try to avoid this later on.

I do have to say that even with all the changes my group has gone through, I'm still glad I started it. It has been a real learning experience and has taught me a lot about myself and my expectations of other people. The group looks very different now than it did years ago, but each person has left their mark on us. Whether it's been a past investigation, a different way to do things or even a viewpoint from another perspective, we wouldn't be where we are without all those experiences. And the beauty is that we will continue to evolve and change. We have to in order to survive.

Between technology, theory and the media, the field is moving at light speed and if you can't keep up you will get left behind. When the other founder of the group decided it was time to resign it was completely bittersweet for me. I was excited to finally move the group forward (since we had been in limbo for a few months while things were being decided) but it was also sad to not have her there anymore to run things by. I had to take on the full responsibility of running this group and if I made a mistake there was no one left holding the bag except me.

In starting your own group you also have creative control. Even though we try to shy away from the commercial side of all this, ultimately we are a brand. In order to be successful you have to gain some notoriety, whether it's good or bad will be up to you. It will help you book investigations and get into places if you have a presence in the field. In my group, we always joke about flying under the radar.

We don't like to be out there in the mix of the para-drama that goes on around us (although it often finds its way to us anyway). We prefer to let our investigative style speak for itself. For us, it's never been about getting famous and being on TV. We have always just wanted to help people and this has kept us much more grounded than other groups we know.

But if this all sounds like a bit too much for you, finding an existing group to join may be a better option. The perks of joining a group are that you will have less responsibility and will be able to have more fun. You won't have to be concerned with all the day to day issues that come up and if you have a good founder you won't even know half the stuff that they are dealing with. Your blood pressure will be lower and you will have much less stress in your life.

In joining an existing group the biggest concern is that you find one that has the same beliefs you do. For example, it could make for very awkward conversations if you don't believe in orbs and your group does. You may think it is just dust in that photo and everyone else thinks it's a great piece of evidence. If your group believes in provoking and they're making you uncomfortable, that will make for a very unpleasant investigation. The bottom line here is to not make a full commitment until you are sure the group is the right one for you. It may help to ask the group if they have any kind of trial or probationary period, so that you don't get in over your head.

In my group we have a training period that varies based on the person. I like to sit down and have a conversation with a potential member and see how much time they can realistically devote to the group. Do they have any special talents that can bring something useful to the group? What made them interested in ghost hunting and what do they hope to get out of it? These are the kinds of questions you should be asked when you are looking for a group to join.

If it seems too easy to join and there aren't any expectations of you, more than likely the group itself has some issues. You should be able to tell how well put together they are from those first few contacts. You should also do some research yourself. Go to their website, if they have one, and look at what kind of information they post. Do they have a vision or a mission statement posted? Can you look at their evidence or places they've investigated? Does the site look professional or is it covered in floating skulls and photos of graveyards? How seriously do they take themselves? Do they seem professional or does this seem like more of a hobby for them? You can learn a lot beforehand by doing some leg work. This will also help you formulate better questions to ask them about their group during those first contacts.

When trying to join a group you have to sell yourself the best you can. You want to show that having you in the group would be an asset to them, not a hindrance. What can you bring to the table? Do you have any community connections or perhaps your good with computers? Chances are that well established groups are getting inquires for membership on a regular basis. You have to figure out what will set you apart from the others.

You should also have a general idea of how much time you have to devote to the group. Most groups will have a monthly or bi-monthly meeting that members are expected to attend. This may or may not be that important depending on the group. In my group it's very important because this is where we confirm upcoming investigations, discuss issues or concerns and address equipment demands. It also helps to keep everyone on the same page since there may be times when you don't investigate as much as you do other times of the year. November, December and January tend to be the slowest months for us due to holidays and of course the weather. Living in Buffalo, NY adds its own challenges to traveling to investigative sites during winter months, and we travel a lot.

Always keep in mind that as much as you are trying to figure out if a group is right for you, they are doing the same thing from their end. In my experience sometimes it works out great and sometimes it doesn't. No matter what happens, just try to remain positive and professional. You may have to try a few groups before you find that perfect fit, but it will be worth it. My group is like a second family and even though we don't always see eye to eye, in the end we all believe in the purpose of what we are doing.

The Parlor of the Summit House in Lockport, NY. One of PRONE's first investigations.

5. WHAT MAKES A GOOD INVESTIGATOR?

Good investigators are not hard to find if you know what you're looking for. Whenever we do presentations or interviews, people often ask what makes a good investigator. Keep in mind that these are the qualities that I look for, depending on the fundamentals of the group, these things can vary. The characteristics that I look for can be found in each one of my investigators. They are all unique in their own ways but they all have some of the same traits too.

If you are going to start a group it's important to know what you're looking for in your members. Don't just invite your friends and family members in. I have seen this cause undue stress, not to mention that it typically doesn't work out. Look at this like a business and therefore try to treat everyone the same. Sometimes it can be difficult to decide who goes on which investigations or how to address concerns with someone not pulling their weight. This will be even harder to address if it's your friend or family member you're having difficulties with.

If you do choose to include your friends or family members, I would suggest having an open conversation about roles and expectations. This may not help avoid all the potential issues, but at least it will help some and could possibly save a relationship down the line. I know this might seem a bit melodramatic but being an active investigative group does take its toll. If you keep this is mind you will be better prepared when issues arise.

One of the most important components to making a good investigator is having someone who is non-judgmental. This is important because you will be dealing with clients and contacts from varying backgrounds and with different cultural and religious beliefs. It's not our job as investigators to decide if a client/contact is to blame for what is going on at a particular location. If they used a Ouija board and then activity kicked up, it's good information for us to know but it doesn't mean we won't help them. Also you shouldn't go into a location offering to do a blessing or a house cleansing (especially if you don't have training from a professional) if you don't have the same beliefs as the people who live or work there. This is very important. If you have a family with Christian beliefs, you aren't going to go and offer a Wiccan house cleansing. Part of being a group clients can trust is that you know who to contact if you can't help.

You also want to look for investigators who are skeptics. I know that this may sound counter-productive, but it's also very important. Keep in mind there is a big difference between skeptics and cynics. Cynics are not people you want in your group because they are so sure that none of this stuff exists, they will only hinder your team. On the other hand, having a healthy amount of skepticism will only strengthen your team and help you remain objective.

If you will be using a scientific approach, you always want to look for the logical explanation first. Being skeptical is a necessary quality. If there are reports of a door always slamming shut, then trying to recreate that first will help you rule out any non-paranormal activity and save your team from investigating a claim that can be explained. This is invaluable because it may be the only time you are at this particular location and you will want to maximize your time there.

Skepticism is also very important when it comes to evidence review. If you aren't the least bit skeptic you will assume every piece of evidence is paranormal. And I know that sounds a bit crazy but I see it happen more often than not. In my group we all have to come to the same conclusion about a piece of evidence for us to feel comfortable sharing it with our client. It's also important to be skeptical while on investigations. If you aren't you might chalk up certain noises or bangs to being paranormal, but this isn't usually the case. Most likely there is a logical explanation and if you take the extra step to find it you will be helping out your client and putting their minds at ease.

I also look for investigators who are grounded. You have to be able to think logically while on investigations and you have to keep your wits about you. Besides how bad would it look to a client if you ran screaming from their house? There is a difference between being scared and being startled while on an investigation. We do get startled from time to time, this is going to happen. But that is very different from being frightened by every bump and shadow you may experience. Staying grounded is also very important because you may be in areas that are unsafe. If there are hazards in the location, you don't want to panic and try to get out an area too quickly. This could cause injury to you or someone on your team.

I try to find out what strengths an investigator has to figure out how they could best help the team. Perhaps someone is good with technology or they love to do research. It's important to know what people are good at and help them find their niche in the group. This is sometimes very easy to do and other times someone may have to try a few different things to figure out what they are best at.

Another important trait is to find investigators who are well rounded. This means that they have a basic knowledge of how to handle different situations but that they can also recognize their own limitations. I have much more respect for a person who bows out of an investigation than I do for someone who pushes themselves too far. There is no shame in having to step outside for some air if things become too heavy inside. I expect that members of my team will become "jacks of all trades". We are all still learning and since there is no absolute proof of anything in this field, there are no experts. Being well rounded means you have a sense of self and you understand your capabilities as well as your flaws. Some of us are better at some things than others. That's what makes a great team, the more you know and understand about each other the better you'll be able to handle whatever comes your way.

Finding a balance within your team is also very important. You won't functional well if everyone is an A type personality or if everyone is super shy. If people don't initially click, don't try to force a connection. Sometimes as bad as we want someone to work out, it's just not meant to be. As a founder especially, you have to be good at observing how the group works together and soliciting feedback from team members.

If a group is not getting along, this can impact the outcome of your investigations. If you are brining negative energy into a location, you won't get the same results as other groups who are getting along much better. You also need to have each other's backs, literally and figuratively. I can't stress how important this is. You will only have each other to rely on in dark hallways and in facing criticism from peers. I wish that we are all about building each other up but so many groups are about making themselves look better than everyone else no matter what that takes. The current state of our field is not one of cooperation. I truly hope that is not always the case, but only time will tell.

Finally I wanted to touch on what makes a good founder or team leader. This is just as important since leading is different and requires a different skill set. As a founder you will be expected to wear lots of different hats and sometimes more than one at a time. It's not always the most popular role and it is the hardest. You can expect not everyone to agree with you and you will make mistakes. It's often a thankless job but it's also the most essential.

If you are a procrastinator, don't run a group. Everyone will be relying on you to book, coordinate and follow through with everything and if you drop the ball there is no one else to blame, you will simply let your group down. No one will follow you if it's not worth it for them. You have a responsibility as a leader to do just that, lead. Some qualities that I feel are important is to be organized, be a good listener and to have a clear vision to follow. Being a good public speaker is a more recent quality that has become important also. I often say that there are no experts in this field so you shouldn't be expected to have all the answers, but it does help to have a basic understanding of the fundamentals of the field.

Having the ability to network is also an important factor for a founder. You have to feel comfortable reaching out to others because you never know when that will produce your next lead or provide you with help down the line. Attending other meetings and functions outside of your immediate group is the best way to do this. Having a good grasp on what your group stands for will help you make connections that are long lasting. You should be able to talk about what makes your group unique and give someone a general idea of your standards.

Depending on the makeup of your team, you may choose to assign roles to your investigators. This can often be helpful for the founder in trying to manage the day to day operations of a paranormal group. Part of being a good leader is to play up others strengths and to be able to recognize your own short comings. There are definitely certain things my members are better at than me and by assigning set responsibilities; it takes some of the pressure off. If you find yourself struggling this may be helpful to you too.

6. ROLES AND EXPECTATIONS OF MEMBERS

In looking at how to assign roles to investigators, I would suggest playing to their strengths. Do you have people who are better at documenting and paperwork or people who are better at making connections and figuring out tech? There is a place for everyone if you know what to look for in fitting someone in. It's also important to stress that every role is important to how the group runs overall.

By assigning roles to team members, it also allows people the opportunity to make a commitment they feel comfortable with.

Case Manager Cheryl doing some research in Gettysburg, PA.

If someone is doing something they enjoy they will be more apt to put forth the extra effort it may take. Having a set role also helps to ensure everyone pulls their weight. If you notice that certain responsibilities are consistently falling through the cracks, it makes it much easier to deal with rather than having everyone blame each other. Accountability to yourself and to each member is the key to having a successful group. There are a various roles to look at in a group and depending on what your group chooses to focus on these will vary. I'm going to touch on ones that I use and a few that are typical for most groups.

First and foremost having a person who is tech savvy is very important. This role is a much needed one and is always evolving. When looking at someone to fill this role, they should be well versed in the tech your group uses. They should have a working knowledge of set up, use and breakdown for each piece of equipment. It's also helpful if your tech person keeps up with the latest gadgets and gizmos for use in our field. I'm very lucky to have a tech guy who is also able to make equipment if we have a need or idea to try something new.

The tech person should be on each walkthrough in order to gage which equipment will work best for the environment you are investigating. This is very important because depending on the environment certain equipment may be useful while others will be completely useless. It won't help to bring a full DVR system if there is no power source at the location. Without tech you have no evidence and without evidence you can't expect to help a client. In my group we try to purchase large items like the DVR, a TV and cameras as a group. We all chip in to purchase the equipment and it stays with the group. Individual members are encouraged to purchase their own personal equipment and they are responsible for those items.

Depending on the size of your group you may have more than one person assigned to tech. If this is the case I would suggest that you appointment one person as the Tech Manager. It's important to have one person be the overall contact. This ensures good communication and a delegation of duties so that everyone plays a role but things also don't get over looked. My group is small enough that this is not always needed. I also have new investigators spend a lot of time with our Tech Manager so that they learn the skills they need to be able to set up and break down our equipment in the appropriate manner. We do follow a specific protocol to set up and break down and this routine helps to ensure everyone is able to do each job.

The job of the Historian is important to allow us to have a basic understanding of where we are headed and what we may encounter. Each case is different and has certain history that should be respected and acknowledged. Having a basic history on a given location can also help improve your investigation. For instance, if you find out the site you are investigating was once a stop on the Underground Railroad, you can gear your EVP sessions to ask questions relevant to that experience. This will also be helpful information with trying things like the Singapore Theory. (If you are unaware this is the theory of recreating an environment through props, music, speech, etc. to reflect what that environment was like for the spirits you are trying to contact.)

The Historian has to be good at researching and organizing the information they gather. The deeper they dig, the more information you have, the better prepared your group will be. You may also uncover information the property owner was unaware of. This is not uncommon, especially in sites that are very old. Often property changes hands so many times that not all details are passed on. The Historian should also have good people skills since they may have to contact others in order to gain information. Sometimes people are reluctant to talk depending on their circumstances. If you have someone on your team who is approachable, a thorough note taker and a good listener, you have the makings of a great Historian. Do you want to keep a record of the investigations you and your group have conducted? Do you think it's important to follow up with a client afterwards? If so, a Case Manager would be a good idea for your group. They will be able to act almost as a Historian for your own group.

Going into a location for the first time there is certain information that we gather such as EMF readings and claims of the site. Being able to go back and compare this information to future investigations allows a case study to evolve. Putting someone in charge of collecting this information will help the group stay organized and build on the science of this field by looking for correlation in the data collected.

Another role of the Case Manager should be to record the personal experiences (if any) a group has on a particular investigation. This information will come in handy in talking to the client, comparing past investigations, looking for patterns and also in reviewing evidence. It's important to note personal experiences when they occur to see if there is any correlation with physical evidence. It lends more creditability to a personal experience when an EVP or a temperature change occurs along with it. Recording this information is also important in disproving claims or debunking them.

If you do the walk through and note drafts in a certain area, an uneven floor or a door that swings easily, this will prevent the group from wasting time investigating these things when there is a logical explanation. Having these occurrences recorded will also help other groups that may investigate or even your own if you go back to the location at another time.

The Case Manager is also responsible to gather information post investigation so that you can present the most through report possible to the client. Some groups don't count personal experiences as evidence and we don't either unless we have some way to back them up. The Case Manager is important in this process. After the investigation it's their responsibility to gather the information from other members and compile it to see if there was any correlation between personal experiences and evidence found. If we can show a client correlation between a cold spot that was noted and a personal experience someone had in the same area, it adds credibility to what happened and may also correlate with what the client themselves may be experiencing.

The last role to discuss is that of the Founder. As I mentioned previously you will be required to wear many hats. In my group I fill in for whoever can't make it to a particular investigation. This means sometimes I may be setting up tech or taking readings on a walkthrough. It's also my responsibility to schedule investigations and make the contacts. Although I encourage everyone in my group to do the same, the majority of this falls to me. As the Founder, I'm the main contact. My group also has monthly meetings, which I schedule and coordinate. I also go to each walkthrough and initial client meeting and schedule and attend each reveal we do.

I coordinate the paperwork, keep it organized, make and update forms and ensure the clients we work with are comfortable with us as a group. It can be very unnerving letting people you don't know into your own home or business, especially under these circumstances, so I always spend as much time as needed answering their questions and going over the expectations for each investigation. I also try to stay up on what's new and innovative in the field so I can help my group stay on the cusp of what we do. We have a research society that we started a few years back, whose main focus is to learn about topics from each other. Every month has a topic and every member is expected to research the topic and present information on it to the group. This has been very helpful and informative and the more knowledge we have, the more knowledge we can pass on to our clients.

There are certain responsibilities that every member of the group has, including me. These are common things that are tedious and have to done on a regular basis; evidence review is the main one. Every member is expected to go through the evidence they have collected in a timely manner and get what they have (if anything) out to our Tech Manger so he can put it all together for the client. We have a set way we review evidence and everyone is aware of these procedures so there is consistency from investigator to investigator.

Everyone is also expected to attend meetings, investigations and events on a regular basis. This is to ensure that everyone pulls their weight and that the work to fun ratio is the same for everyone. Believe me; it can make for a very awkward meeting when members feel that certain people are not meeting their responsibilities to the group. It makes it much easier to deal with these types of issues if there is an expectation of members to the group and to each other.

Some groups charge dues or membership fees, this is not something that my group does. We each have our own set of equipment as well as equipment that belongs to the group, but we try to split the costs of expenses evenly between each of us. This makes purchasing larger items much easier and it gives everyone a stake in the group. Because we do things this way we don't have a treasurer by any means, but this may be a role you will need to fill if you choose to charge for membership or collect dues. In doing this, it will give your group a pot of money to pull from depending on what you will need. Some groups use the funds to pay for travel expenses or to buy equipment but this situation can get sticky if people don't pay or travel more than others. However you choose to work it out make sure the members of your group are comfortable with it so no one feels like they are being taken advantage of.

In order to keep things harmonious make sure each member understands how these roles will work and what you will expect from them. I have found that giving people particular responsibilities has been the most effective way to delegate duties and ensure everyone feels included. A lot of groups will also talk about "lead investigators". I consider everyone on my team to be a lead investigator so we don't use this term. The only exception is when a new member starts out we do consider them an "investigator in training" until they learn the different roles, but this is only mentioned internally and the length of time someone is training depends on many factors. In my group we all decide when a person is no longer training. I like to get everyone's input since the new trainee shadows each one of them to learn about what they do.

By shadowing the other members of the group, it also gives the trainee an opportunity to see where they fit best also. Maybe they discover that they like learning about the history the best or learning about the latest piece of equipment. You will get more productivity out of your group members if they enjoy what they do.

Roles of investigators can be determined by the unique circumstances of your group. If you are going to start a group, think about the overall vision. Are you going to be a scientific based group or will you be less tradtional? If you have a direction to go in determining the roles will be much easier. And most importantly, don't forget to play to peoples strengths. This will allow for better overall function of your group and happier members who are willing to go the extra mile.

Tech Manager Rob at an event at the Buffalo Historical Society

7. CODES OF CONDUCT

Codes of Conduct outline what you expect from your group members and how the fundamentals of your group will apply, basically they are the rules. These can be decided by you, as the Founder, or by the group itself but no matter who decides on them, it's imperative that everyone abides by them. Your rules can be as intricate or as simple as you like, it all depends on the flavor of your group. I'm going to talk about the codes of conduct we use and about why we abide by them.

First and foremost I expect that everyone in the group will respect each other and our clients. This should go without having to be said, but it's important to hold each other accountable to it. There is enough drama in this field already and there is no need to have it in your own group too. You need to be able to count on each other, after all you will be investigating in potentially dangerous conditions from time to time and everyone should want to look out for each other. Try to remember to be sensitive to clients no matter what you may think about their claims. Give them the benefit of the doubt unless you can disprove what they claim. This is important because how you are perceived by the public can make or break your reputation.

For example, PRONE does a lot of conventions and events and we were at an event when a woman showed one of my team members a photo of what she claimed were orbs. As a group we don't believe in orbs per say and think that 99% of these types of photos are dust, bugs or moisture, but it doesn't mean it's not possible to have an actual orb in a photo. The woman wanted an investigators opinion and boy did she get it. This investigator who is no longer with our group (by their choice) got into a heated discussion about the validity of orbs and basically told this woman the photo was nothing. She seemed very upset by this because she had convinced herself it was a deceased member of her family.

In these types of situations you have to respect the client. Nothing says you have to agree with them but be sensitive. Keep your cool in dealing with situations like this because you are presenting your group. I usually thank a person for sharing and gently give them possible explanations. If they walk away still thinking that piece of dust is Uncle Bill, let them! Remember there are NO experts in this field. Unless you were there and took the photo yourself you can't say if it is or isn't something paranormal.

Sometimes you will have clients that seem less than stable (we'll talk more about this later) but no matter how far off their rocker they seem they still deserve respect and should be treated with such. It's important to remember that each individual person represents the group as a whole. Many times when I hear complaints about other groups it's always "that guy from (insert name here)", it's not usually "John". One bad apple can spoil the bunch and will so don't be that guy!

I expect that each member of the group will conduct themselves with the upmost professionalism when representing PRONE. This means that when we are in public as a group or on investigations, everyone will follow the codes of conduct. Nothing hurts a groups' reputation more than infighting and being un-professional. You are bound to have disagreements about things or have issues from time to time, but handle these at a meeting or on a personal level, never in front of a client or in a public forum. This kind of behavior can severely tarnish the public persona of the group and you will work hard to build yours. In a field of so many it's hard to distinguish yourself from all the others. You have control over what you are remembered for.

Truthfulness is an absolute value that each member must abide by. We have to be able to trust each other for the evidence we get, to investigating together, to personal experiences. If you can't say you trust your team members how do you expect a client to trust you? I have to know that every member of PRONE will conduct themselves in a trust worthy manner. If someone sends me an EVP to listen to, I have to be able to trust the source. If someone tells me they saw a shadow down a hallway, I have to be able to feel that they are being truthful. I feel very lucky to work with a group of people who are fine with saying that they didn't get any evidence from an investigation as opposed to people who try to say things are paranormal when they aren't. If I'm going to sit down with a client and go over the evidence that was captured, I have to feel just as comfortable presenting a group members' EVP as I would one I captured myself.

Appearance is not a major factor for me, but there are a few standards that PRONE has. I don't think you have to get crazy with this and I've seen other groups say everything from no tattoos showing to having full blown dress codes. I care about two things. The first is that you dress appropriately for the investigations so that you are safe and comfortable. This means no flip flops or open toed shoes since we are often in places that have broken glass, uneven floors, no electricity or other possible hazardous conditions.

I would also suggest that you bring a first aid kit on investigations, just in case. I want everyone to be comfortable too so causal clothing is a must. It's very distracting if you are dressed inappropriately for yourself and for your fellow investigators. This also seems like it should be common sense, but you'd be surprised! I've been on public investigations with people wearing high heels and skirts. Nothing dampers an investigation like a twisted ankle, so wear comfortable appropriate shoes!

No one cares what you look like and most of the time you're in the dark anyway! Also it's important to not wear anything that will distract your fellow investigators. Don't wear heavy perfume or cologne since this may mask other scents that could be associated with the paranormal. If a client claims to smell peppermint when sensing someone is around, you could miss this if your fellow investigator is wearing heavy perfume or cologne. Also be aware of the accessories you chose to wear. Earring that dangle and make noise will drive investigators crazy, especially when trying to review evidence. Just use good judgment when getting ready to head out to a location.

The second thing is that you wear something (preferably a t-shirt) with the PRONE logo on it. This is important so that there is some uniformity between the investigators. Your group will look more professional to the client than if everyone just showed up in regular everyday clothes. You want your client to feel that you take investigating seriously and if you present yourselves as a team, you will be seen that way.

Each team member should be familiar with your groups' mission statement or philosophy. Where does your group stand on controversial subjects like provoking and charging fees? Do you think orbs are the real deal or just dust? It's important that each team member represents the group in a consistent manner. Not everyone has to agree on every subject but there should be a general consensus on the main issues. If you believe in crossing spirits over, PRONE is not the group for you, but if you like to try to debunk claims you'd fit right in.

Another rule we have is that we NEVER investigate alone. There are many reasons why we abide by this and it is something I take very seriously. We use the buddy system in order to keep everyone safe and to ensure we know where people are. We are almost always in the dark and often times in huge locations, I can't tell you the sense of panic I feel when someone is unaccounted for, not to mention the time is takes away from the investigation to find them.

A few years ago we did two investigations at Waverly Hills in Louisville, KY. If you are familiar with the location you know that the building is vast. It has numerous floors and areas that are open to the elements. Waverly was a tuberculosis hospital and had open areas where they would wheel patients out because they thought that fresh air would cure them. On our first night there we explored many of these areas and noted that they just dropped off at the edge. It was a very far drop to the ground level and needless to say we were very careful.

The second night one of my investigators told us she was going out for a smoke and would be back in a few minutes. Since this was a hunt with lots of other people we were fine with her going to the designated area alone. We noticed she was not back after about a half an hour and went to this area to look for her, but she wasn't there. No one we asked remembered seeing her and we had no way to contact her since she didn't have a walkie talkie or a phone. I was fearful that something had happened to her and set off to search. After a very stressful 45 minutes we located her talking to the owner of the building. I was very glad she was ok, but very upset that hadn't checked in. Not only did we waste almost an hour that we could have been investigating, we were worried and imagining that something tragic may have happened. The lesson here is always let your team members know where you are! Stay in contact.

The other reason you shouldn't investigate alone is that you may have something happen like seeing a shadow or being touched and have no one there to corroborate the experience. We say all the time that it's so much better when someone else sees/feels the same thing you do. I was conducting an investigating in the basement area of Rolling Hills Asylum and it was just me and another investigator when we heard a little girl call "mommy". We were lucky to have had a recorder going and caught this EVP, but if I was there by myself I would have second guessed what I heard.

The natural skeptic in me would have come up with 10 reasons that I didn't just hear what I think I did. Having that second person there (along with the recorder) lent credibility to my experience. It also helps to debunk things. There have been times when I thought I heard something but it was not confirmed by the other person or could be explained.

As a group, we don't carry cell phones during investigations for a few reasons. First, the phones are a distraction. Texting your friend or updating your Facebook status when on an investigation is not professional. When you're on a break or stepping out for some air, then it's time to check in or text. The other reason is that the phones, even when off, ping the closest cell towers on a regular basis. This can mess with equipment like the K2 meter and give off false readings. If you have to have the phone with you, leave it back at the base area or in your car. I have seen K2 meters go off right before a phone rings or receives a text message and if you don't know that there's a connection you can easily misinterpret this as evidence.

Confidentiality is a code that we take very seriously. We have had the privilege of investigating some very prominent places in our local community and as much as I'd love to name names, I can't due to our confidentiality agreements with these locations. We give each client the opportunity to keep what we do at their location confidential and while most clients allow us to fully disclose what we get, some don't. Being able to keep quiet is priceless to a client.

Sometimes clients are worried about how the community will react or what their neighbors will think and it's important to be able to give them piece of mind. There is still a certain stigma about the paranormal out there and not everyone is open minded to the possibilities of life after death. Being able to provide a client with complete anonymity has helped us book investigations at some pretty incredible places. Sometimes this can be very hard to do, especially when the bragging rights alone would be crazy but it's not worth ruining your groups reputation for a moment of smudge satisfaction. You can share those experiences with your other group members who have been sworn to secrecy.

Lastly, there needs to be a clear idea of each investigators level of commitment and dedication to the group, themselves and the field. Your intentions in investigating should come from a pure and humble place. We are not special; anyone can pick up a flashlight and do what we do. The knowledge we gain should be shared not coveted and kept secret. We have a responsibility to educate each other and the public as we learn more and more.

Alison Smith

8. SHOULD GROUPS CHARGE FEES?

To charge or not to charge

From time to time ideas in the paranormal field come up that ignite a bit of controversy and whether or not to charge fees for investigating has become a hot button issue. Let me say right from the beginning that I am not and will never be in support of charging a fee to a client. Now before you say but what about the cost of equipment and travel? And after all, aren't we providing a service? Don't we deserve some compensation? My answer is simple; in my opinion it's unethical to charge a fee to perform a service that is entirely based on theory and requires no special skill.

I am aware that other services such as psychics/mediums and energy healers accept payment for what they do, and I don't feel that this is unethical. They also tend to offer a set price for their services rendered and most often it's their full time profession and has a specific skill to it as opposed to it being a hobby. The client is also willingly going to seek these people out for spiritual guidance and not expecting physical proof of anything. They have faith that they are getting guidance or healing so they feel validated.

I can tell you from my own personal experience, as a Reiki practitioner (Reiki is a form of energy healing) that I had to go through extensive training to be able to offer Reiki to others and there is payment involved. This may not always be monetary but it's something so that there is an understanding that a service has been rendered. The difference to me is that anyone could become a ghost hunter tomorrow but not everyone can realign some ones chakras without any training.

In looking at this topic, there a few questions I want to raise and let you figure out for yourself which side of the fence you fall on. We have discussed throughout this book about the importance of building your reputation and having your own identity, knowing where you stand on topics will help you establish your own code of conduct. I'm not going to tell you that you should or shouldn't charge, I'm just going to share my feelings and maybe help you think about it from a different perspective.

Right now groups are charging clients everything from flat rate fees, to hourly charges to extra fees for dealing with negative spirits. There is even a group I came across that charges a set fee to "cross spirits over". Now you could make the argument that this requires a skill so there for a fee can be charged, but I have many doubts about the validity of this particular claim in the first place. I find it disturbing that anyone would "guarantee" to a client that they could rid them of a ghost by forcing them into the light. This preys on the emotions a person is having and makes them dependent on you to help solve the problem. This is a direct contradiction to how PRONE does things. We always empower the client to have the confidence to rid themselves of a spirit if they can't co-exist.

We work with the client on a few techniques that they can employ to take back their space and put up boundaries to feel more comfortable. We don't force things into the light because first of all, we can't communicate directly with ghosts. If we could, we would have a lot better EVP sessions they we do and probably more answers to our questions about matters like life after death. Also how do you know a spirit should go to the light in the first place? What if they committed a horrible crime or weren't religious? The more we dive into this idea the stickier it gets. We shouldn't presume to know what the religious views of a ghost were while they were alive. If you can communicate directly with the ghost to ask them these questions than why are you hunting them in the first place?

Also it makes me wonder if claims like these come with a money back guarantee. If you claim to cross a spirit over and rid the client of them and the issues continue does the client get to call you back a second or third time free of charge? Do you get the fifth removal free? Do you charge by the EVP or photo/video evidence?

I'm obviously being a bit sarcastic but doesn't this whole idea sound a little bit farfetched? If you're like me and can't talk directly to ghosts than how do you know if you're dealing with Aunt Betty who likes a chair in a particular place and keeps moving it or a demon hell bent on scaring the crap out of you? In my opinion you can't. If we run into a situation that seems like it may need more attention than we can give it, we call in someone with more experience. There is nothing wrong with this. I'd always rather play it safe than make matters worse by trying to help when we aren't qualified to do so.

Sometimes clients may want to offer some form of payment for the investigation you've conducted. I have taken donations before if this is the case. The difference is that the donation is not contingent in any way of helping a client. The donations always go to pay for equipment, food, travel or operating costs and in all the years I've been doing this I can count on one hand the number of donations we have accepted. Most times its simple things like having food at a home investigation that we feel is payment enough. If you say that you want to help people, then you have to help all people, not just the ones who can afford to pay.

There have been a few times we have held events and public hunts at specific locations and charged a fee per person, but we have done this strictly to fundraise for that location. People often complain about paying fees to be able to investigate certain locations. I agree that sometimes the fees are expensive but it also costs large amounts of money to run some of these locations. There are groups that will hold functions similar to this and pocket the majority of the money. It probably won't be public knowledge about how the funds are to be distributed so if you feel uncomfortable with not knowing whether or not your money is going to the location itself, you can always ask. You may not get a straight answer and that should be a red flag that the group is probably profiting more than the location. If you feel private investigation fees are too costly, you can always see if the location offers a public investigation fee, which most due. This is usually much cheaper although you will have to deal with more people then also.

I think my biggest concern in charging clients for investigating is that it will be difficult to draw the line with other things paranormal. Will we start charging people to rid their lands of Big Foot and Chupacabras? If you decide you are going to charge then put in writing what you are going to do along with the fees. Be responsible and make sure you discuss this up front with the client before doing any investigation. Outline exactly what your fees cover such as travel expenses and equipment costs, that way you can justify to the client why payment is needed. If the client decides not to allow you to investigate due to the fee, offer them other alternatives. If a client is in sincere need it would be unethical to leave them high and dry because they may not be willing or able to pay you.

Not all people in the paranormal community believe that charging fees is an ethical issue. It's also not an issue that will easily go away and people will probably never agree, but for me it comes down to my conscious. My conscious wouldn't allow me to turn someone away who truly needed help simply because they couldn't pay for it. There are other things you and your team can do to raise funds if you need to. Having experience does count for something and should be something a client considers when locating an investigative team, but charging fees can be misleading. If a client thinks in the normal consumer mode of paying the most means they get the best team, they could be sadly mistaken.

If you plan to charge a fee you should consider what makes your team different from another that doesn't charge? Do any of your members have special skills? Is there a specific type of haunting your team specializes in? These are the kinds of factors that make you different. Don't get me wrong, I not saying that my team doesn't have specific expertise because we don't charge. All I'm saying is that if you plan to, you should have a solid reason for doing so other than "we deserve it".

Also keep in mind that if you are going to charge fees you will have to have set policies in place about cancellations, refunds and so on. If this seems like more hassle than it's worth, that's probably because it is! Running teams, investigations and dealing with the drama are all very time consuming and draining, why add on more stressor to the list. Soon this won't be any fun and you'll be completely burnt out and even getting paid won't be enough to make you want to continue. Keep it light and if your group really needs money for equipment or travel, have a bake sale.

9. PAPERWORK, FORMS & DOCUMENTATION

I know what you're thinking, I just said keep it light and keep it fun and here I am writing a chapter about paperwork. I know that sounds contradictory but I'll explain how it's not. What I want you to take away from this chapter is that if you do some of the leg work upfront, it'll be easier on you, your team and the client, not to mention how it will improve your evidence. You might think that paperwork is a pain and it's too much work but with a few key forms you'll see it's much easier than it sounds.

Also keep in mind that the paperwork I'm going to talk about grew out of necessity for us. We didn't start out using these forms but over the years we found that we were asked for the same things over and over and that we really wanted a uniform way to keep case files from the places we frequented.

It's also important to remember that you can delegate who does what in your group. You don't have to take on all the responsibility of completing these forms and you shouldn't! Let everyone get involved and have an equal stake in it. Also you'll want to have different perspectives and impressions throughout the investigation and if all your info comes from you alone, you will have nothing to compare it to.

The first form I think you should consider is an introduction letter. This can be a simple paragraph or so about who you are as a group, your mission statement, places you've investigated and probably most important, that you will provide references upon request. Potential clients will feel more comfortable if you have references that are current and are willing to talk about their experiences with your group. If you can provide references (I would try to have at least 3) it shows that you are serious and that you have some experience and will put the client at ease.

The introduction letter should also contain your contact information and where they can locate more information about your group, like a website. This information will allow them to check you out on their own time without the pressure of a face to face meeting. Not everyone is still willing or comfortable talking about the paranormal, especially if you are contacting a public place. You may want to include a brochure or a card for easy reference and contact information.

If you are brand new and don't have any references to list there are a few ways to gain the experience you'll need. You can start by booking a few investigations at a local place that offers private and/or public investigations. Usually there will be an owner or a member of the staff present during your investigations and ask them to come out and observe your group. Invite them to work with your group so they can see firsthand how you do things.

After 2-3 investigations, ask them for a reference. I have a form already created that can be easily filled out. It's basically a blanket statement about our professionalism and then I leave some blank lines at the bottom for the contact to write in any additional information. I also have a check box to see if they would be willing to be contacted by a potential client and if so, how they would prefer the contact (email, phone call, etc.).

Another way to get a reference is to volunteer your time to a worthy cause. Our group does public reveals and lectures for free for certain sites we investigate regularly. We also participate in numerous fund-raisers throughout the year. This can be a great way to build relationships in your community and allow people to get to know you and what you do. The more you give back the more you'll get and you never know where your next investigation lead may come from.

The next form we use is a Client Intake form. This form is a few pages long and is a questionnaire that is partly filled out by us and partly by the client themselves. We have had to develop this because we found that not all clients are honest about their experiences. There are many reasons for this which can be anything from trying to gain notoriety to mental illness, but having these set series of questions help us weed out who is really in need of help.

ABOVE ALL WE SEEK THE TRUTH

To Whom It May Concern:

Please allow this letter to serve as an introduction to PRONE (Paranormal Researchers of Niagara and Erie). PRONE is a well established and professional group of paranormal researchers whose purpose it is to investigate claims of paranormal type activity. PRONE has investigated many establishments and private residences and will provide letters of reference upon request. Please see below for a list of some of the places we have conducted past investigations:

- The Summit House, Lockport, NY
- The Knickerbocker Inn, Linesville, PA
- The USS Sullivan, Buffalo, NY
- The Palmyra Museum, Palmyra, NY
- The Buffalo Central Terminal, Buffalo, NY
- The Valentown Museum, Valentown, NY
- Mahoney Doll Gallery/Bertie Hall, Ontario, CA
- Iron Island Museum, Lovejoy, NY
- Waverly Hills Sanatorium, Louisville, KY
- Rolling Hills Asylum, E. Bethany, NY
- Eastern State Penitentiary, Philadelphia, PA
- Mansfield State Prison, Mansfield, OH
- Buffalo Central Library, Buffalo, NY

We would love the opportunity to investigate your establishment as well. We thrive on conducting ourselves with the utmost respect and professionalism possible. We are more than willing to provide additional information if necessary. If you would be willing to allow us to come to your establishment for the purpose of investigation or if you just require more information please feel free to contact me at info@prone.org or you can contact me directly at

Thank you for your consideration of this matter.

Sincerely,

Copy of PRONEs Introduction Letter

We usually do the questionnaire with all the adults in the house and have them write in their own words about what they've been experiencing. These personal experiences can help us narrow down where we will need to set up the equipment and possible hotspots, but will also give us some insight into potential explanations.

For example, if a family reports that most of them feel uncomfortable in the basement of their house (like someone is there or watching them) we know this may be due to high EMF and that it could easily be explained away. There have been times when EMF is not the issue, but that's why you use the equipment and always rule out the logical first. The intake form is also great for case files if you choose to create them. If you get called back in 6 months later, you'll have a written record of what took place last time including the claims. This will be very helpful since our memories can be tainted and not always accurate.

The next form that I developed is probably the most important, it's the Investigation Protocol. This is a step by step description of how we run an investigation and what the client can expect. It clearly outlines the steps we take to schedule, set up and conduct our investigations. We post a link to this on our website so that any potential client can look at it ahead of time to get an idea of what to expect. I decided to write the protocol because I would often be asked the same types of questions before each investigation. Also I was afraid I would leave something out or forget to mention a key factor when I was trying to describe the service to people. This makes it a lot easier and then people can take it with them to have to refer back to later on.

As the years have gone on, people have been exposed to a lot more TV shows and have a better idea about how the typical investigation works but we will still get people once in a while who don't watch the shows and don't really have an interest in the paranormal, they just happen to live or work in a haunted location. In these cases the protocol helps to set their mind at ease that there won't be 10 people invading their house demanding to speak to demons.

If you are not planning on starting a group and are just looking to join one, it's still important to know about your group documents, what they do and what they are used for. This is especially true if they claim to be a group that is scientific or research based. If they don't actually document anything they do and make these claims, this should be a red flag to you that things are not as they seem. If you are looking to join more of a metaphysical based group, then this is a moot point for you. Just ask some questions when considering a potential group and use your gut, if it doesn't feel right, it's probably not the right one for you.

The last form that we use is also the most important for our research. In order to keep track of what happens during and after the investigation, we needed a way to document what took place on a consistent basis. This is why the Case File form came into use. The Case File form has two parts. The first has the basic information of the date, time and location, but it also documents prior claims, the EMF walkthrough and any initial impressions. This means what we notice when we first come into the location, is it loud? Is there a lot of traffic? Are the neighbors close? Is the building old? Sometimes you may get a "heavy" feeling or become uneasy. These may be good clues for us to refer back to later on.

It also has a place to document EVP sessions. This information is important for a few reasons. First it asks for the location of the session and the time frame. These are two things you should document on your recorder but sometimes people forget.

This is also helpful if you will be doing multiple investigations at the same location. You may find that you tend to run sessions in the same parts of a location or that some pattern may emerge over time. It also asks for impressions during the session. Since impressions are based on feeling it's not something that would easily come across on a recording, but if a certain questions produces a change in how the location feels, this is important information to remember. There is also a space to document which investigators were present during the session and if anything unusual took place. Even though we always try to make sure we "tag" our EVP sessions, sometimes we forget and don't make note of everything that happens.

The form should be filled out by at least two investigators since everyone perceives things differently. In having at least two people fill it out you will be able to look at any similarities or differences that you may not have been aware of otherwise. It's also interesting to see if the client has had any of the same experiences or impressions.

After an investigation is over, it's the role of the Case Manager to take this information and compile it into a short summary. The summary will include any physical evidence we discovered as well as our impressions both pre and post investigation. Having this information will allow you to look at the overall picture of what the investigation was like and it may help to classify the type of activity that may be taking place.

If you think this will hinder your investigation and bog it down, I would suggest starting slowly with just a simple pad and a pen. Just jot down what you feel if anything and see if having this insight is helpful to you post investigation. It's very difficult to remember everything that happens during a 5 hour investigation and you don't want to miss an important clue.

Cheryl completing a form during an investigation at The Knickerbocker Hotel in Linesville, PA

94

10. TECH: JUST THE BASICS

In deciding to start ghost hunting the question of equipment is usually the first thing you have to try to figure out. Some items that you will need may seem like common sense but you would be surprised how many people will show up to investigate without any equipment, even a flashlight. How do they expect to see in the dark? On the flip side of this there are always a few people who show up with cases upon cases of very pricy and fancy looking gadgets.

I'm going to try to guide you to the middle of this road. I can honestly tell you that most of the time which equipment you decide to use will not get you better or worse evidence. I've heard some of the best EVPs come from cheap recorders that have been used for many years. As with most things in this field, I suggest you do some research and try out a few models until you find one you are comfortable with. A digital recorder is no good to you if it's too complicated and difficult to use.

Author doing some EVP work at Iron Island Museum in Lovejoy, NY

We are going to discuss the basics here of what you will need to conduct an investigation in a scientific way. We will also touch on a few items we use that are more theory based and less scientific because we like to try new ideas. If you want more in depth information you should consider reading *"Modern Technology in Paranormal Research"* by Rob Gallitto. Rob is the Tech Manager for PRONE and he has a wealth of knowledge. He's conducted a lot of experiments with some of the tech we use and also makes some of our equipment. His book will give you the explanations for, use of and purpose of lots of different kinds of equipment as well as some real life examples of how it's been used on our investigations. After that shameless plug, let's get started...

The most important piece of equipment you should have on every investigation is a flashlight. The flashlight can be used to communicate with ghosts but its most important function is to provide you the ability to walk around safely in the dark. A lot of people will ask us about investigating at night verses the day time and really you can do either. We tend to investigate more at night because locations are closed to the public by then, it's quieter and we all have day jobs. Sometimes locations can be in run down condition and can have hazards like uneven flooring, holes, broken glass, etc. and the last thing you want is a reason to have to use the first aid kit.

There is no right or wrong kind of flashlight to use. I have a few different kinds that I bring and they have different purposes. The ones I use for the purpose of communicating, I don't use as a regular light source and I keep them separate. I keep my Maglite holstered expect when I set it up for the purpose of communication. If you've watched any paranormal show in the last 5 years you've probably seen this done many times. My group is still experimenting with the possible theories of how exactly they work and heat being one of those factors. To eliminate this I don't use it otherwise so the temperature of the inside mechanism stays more neutral.

There is also a certain set of rules that we use when asking questions and will not proceed with a session if the responses we are getting are inconsistent. If we are running a session we will ask the same question in a few different ways. This is an important step for us because if we are getting the same responses it lends credibility to the interaction. If you plan to use the Maglite as a means to communicate, work out how your group will do so.

Having everyone run a session the same way is very important to the integrity of your investigation. If everyone uses a different approach you won't have anything solid to compare from one investigation to the next.

If you believe that the Maglite is flawed and want a more concrete way of communicating, a voice recorder is the next piece of equipment to use. I use both of these in conjunction to ensure I cover as many bases as possible but it's up to you to decide what you're comfortable with. Voice recorders differ in price and function vastly. You don't have to buy the most expensive one for it to be good. In fact, some of the best EVPs I've caught have come from my first inexpensive recorder. Please don't make the mistake of buying one that is so complicated you can't figure out how to work it; this will do you no good. The most important thing to look for is that it has a USB port, without this you won't be able to load the data into your computer which will make it very difficult to share and review your evidence.

Using a voice recorder is a staple while investigating the paranormal and if it malfunctions, it can leave you at a loss for how to proceed. Always remember to ensure you have extra batteries on hand. Battery drain is a real thing, I've experienced it firsthand. Your batteries will also go bad just from leaving them in the equipment over long periods of time so you may want to remove them in between. It's important to note that however long you spend recording, it will take you the same amount of time to go through it. Unless you will have days to review your evidence, you may want to consider running smaller more frequent sessions rather than letting the recorder run for hours on end. Each investigator in my group has a recorder and we use them at different times for this reason.

The next item in your bag should be a camera of some sort. Whether you would rather use a digital camera or a digital camcorder is up to you. Most people already have one or both and may not need to purchase something new. Any digital camera can be used but a camcorder will require a "night shot" function to allow you to see in the dark. Camcorders can be expensive and you may choose to purchase something like this as a group. This is usually what we do with our larger equipment to help defer the cost. If you want to buy a camera specifically for ghost hunting try to find something that is more on the rugged side since you will most likely drop it at some point and besides you'll be in the dark so no one is going to see it anyway.

Almost every member of my group has a digital camera, camcorder or both. One member has a full spectrum camera and the group has a DVR and a set of four cameras that run to it. This may sound like a bit of overkill but sometimes we investigate large buildings and we can't be everywhere so the cameras help to cover areas we may not be able too. The DVR is the first group purchase we made and probably gets used the most, but it's not a necessary piece of equipment. You don't need it to start out and we will still get great evidence from our hand held cameras just as often.

The last piece of equipment is a tossup between two popular items that have the same purpose. Most people think you need an EMF detector and a K2 meter in order to investigate, but you really just need one or the other. I like them both for different reasons and find that I use them equally but others in my group have one or both also. The typical EMF detector will have a digital display that shows you the EMF levels in any given area. Some will also have a temperature gage build in which eliminates the need for a digital thermometer. I prefer to use this on walkthroughs because it gives me a more precise reading than the K2. The K2 seems to be better for communication and interaction with ghosts, maybe they prefer the lights or the K2 just looks more interesting?

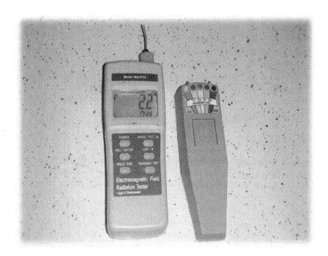

Whatever the reason it seems that it's used more for this purpose them for trying to find EMF levels. K2 meters now also come with built in temperature gages but without a read out it's hard to know what the exact differences are that it's sensing. As with many aspects of ghost hunting it comes down to preference. First decide what you want to use the equipment for and this will help you decide which one will best meet your needs.

There is a lot of equipment out there and the list of what is available is growing every day. Keep in mind that most of these items are fads and will come and go. I'm guilty of jumping on a few of these trends which is why I have laser grids, red flashlights, UV lights and a whole bag of other items I don't use. Learn from my mistakes; be wise about what you spend your money on. Work out what you will buy with your group members so that you can have lots of options with what you will use on different investigations. These are just the basics, as you do more investigations you will have a better idea of what you need. It's also important to remember that you will have to store all your equipment somewhere and will have to lug it back and forth from each location. This can be a workout depending what you bring so only take what you think you will actually use.

**Eastern State Penitentiary where the Hack Shack came in handy
during one of our investigations there.**

11. NON-TRADITIONAL EQUIPMENT AND TOOLS

As you investigate for a while you will be exposed to lots of different types of equipment and some of these may seem very strange at first, but with some trial and error they may become some of your favorites. As with looking at basic equipment, we could just write a book on the nontraditional items, also so we will focus on a few of the more popular ones.

One of my favorite things to do on an investigation is to run a Hack Shack session because you never know what you will get. A Hack Shack is a simple am/fm radio that has been "hacked" by opening up the back and breaking a pin located inside. This allows the radio to continuously cycle through stations and allows ghosts to use the radio to communicate. There are a few different theories on how exactly this works. If you are skeptical about it, I would encourage you to try it out for yourself.

There are a few things we do to ensure we aren't picking up local radio stations. One of the things we do is ask for the spirit to tell us their favorite swear word. This often works and we know that FCC laws don't allow foul language to be used. We also have a particular way that we open and close the session since we are opening up a direct line to communicate; we want to be cautious about what may come through. The Hack Shack does the same thing as a Ghost box, Puck system or programs like Ghost Radar. I prefer the Hack Shack because it doesn't come with a preformed vocabulary or preset phrases. As long as I've been using the Hack Shack I have never heard the same words repeated expect for the typical yes or no. And it can be a bit unnerving to ask it to name someone in the room and without hesitation it mentions your name. Some of the best EVPS we've captured have come from the Hack Shack.

Another great nontraditional tool is your body. How does this work? Well just ask yourself how many times have you walked into a room where it felt like the air was thick? Have you ever turned a corner and felt the hair on the back of your neck stand up? Next time you're out on an investigation or just touring a haunted location, try to let your mind go blank and just see what you can experience. Is the area warm or cold? Does it feel comfortable or does the area make you anxious? Or perhaps you just feel nothing at all. Try to turn off that part of your brain that is always trying to figure things out, always trying to explain away what you can't immediately understand. Just let yourself be in the environment. What you are trying to connect to is the energy that may or may not be there.

An easy way to think about this is to believe (even temporarily) in the idea that all things including spirits are made up of energy. Some may be more intense than others and easier to pick out while some may be weaker and easy to miss. Think about people in your own life, some have huge personalities; some are more shy and reserved. This is the same principle as understanding how energy works from a metaphysical stand point. Your body senses the changes in the energy and produces a physical reaction. If you're sitting in an area that is comfortable and you suddenly get the chills, this could be your body sensing a change in the energy around you. If the air around you seems to change and maybe it becomes thick, or it's harder to breathe, perhaps the energy is no longer pleasant and wants you to leave.

So how can this help you during an investigation? First I want to stress that working with energy takes practice. Also using this technique should not take the place of actual scientific equipment. It's my experience that they go nicely hand in hand. If you feel that cold spot you can check it against the equipment and look for correlation. As I've stated previously, when I investigate I always start with a walkthrough. I take my time to try to get a general feel for the place and make mental notes about how the different areas strike me and what my initial physical reactions are if any. The more you try this the more success you will have with tuning in to what is or isn't there. Some people may catch onto this more quickly than others, but don't get discouraged if this happens to you. Keep trying and it will get easier.

This can help also by narrowing your investigation down to a smaller investigation space. For example, if you are in a large location and feel like there may be something in one area, you can concentrate on that rather than spreading out to try to cover everything else, especially if you have limited time in the location. You may also find a new hot spot since; after all, spirits can travel. What may be considered a hot spot one day might not be the same for you depending on many factors.

It's also important to try not to force a reaction. If you go into a location to investigate with preconceived notions or ideas about it, you will be more apt to have an experience related to that information. Unfortunately I've seen this happen many times. As an example, if you go into a location where children are said to be, you are more likely to hear a child giggle or see a small fleeting shadow because you are expecting it. Your brain will try to relate an experience to something that can be explained. This may be why "spirit children" are often found in locations where children did not frequent or were not known to be.

You may also want to try writing down your initial impressions. It's always a good idea to have a pad and pen with you on an investigation just for this purpose. You may get an idea that will pop into your head that seems to make no sense at the time of the investigation. If this happens, jot it down. It's also a good idea to write down how the area feels to you. When you go to conduct your EMF sweeps you may find the cause to some of what you experienced. Perhaps you felt uneasy in a certain area and find a high concentration of EMF there. Most likely what you felt is your body's reaction to that rather than a ghost. You may want to have a few members of your group do this and then compare notes afterwards to see if any of your impressions were similar.

The point of all this is to use your basic instincts and allow yourself to tune in to your surroundings. As great as all the equipment is, it doesn't make you a better investigator to have all the bells and whistles and it just may make you broke. No piece of equipment is more sensitive than your body is, so trust your feelings and try this out.

Dowsing Rods are also a great tool to use for investigating. They work by honing into the energy in a given area. They can also be used for the purpose of communication by tuning them in prior to starting an investigation. What I mean by this is start with the rods in a neutral position, then ask a question that you know will have a no answer and wait for the rods to cross. Once you establish this ask another question that will have a yes answer and wait for the rods to open wide. You can allocate a cross or open response to either a yes or no, however you want. They can also be used to find the ghosts that may be lingering by pointing in the direction of the energy. I would suggest doing a walkthrough of the area prior to using the rods so you know you aren't honing in to an established source of EMF such as old wiring or an alarm clock on a dresser.

You can ask the rods to cross when they locate the source of the energy they are picking up. This may sound silly if you don't have any experience in using the rods, but like most tools or equipment it takes some getting used to. The most important point to remember in using the rods is to let them do the work. Hold them lightly and evenly in both hands and follow where they lead.

Along these lines of locating energy another tool to try is a pendulum. This is usually made up of a stone of weight on the end of a chain or string. Like the rods it can be used to ask yes and no questions. First establish which way you would like it to move

pendalum

for each response. Hold the end of the chain or string in your hand and let the stone or weight hang freely. Wait till there is no movement and then ask your question. I use a north south response for yes and an east west response for no, similar to shaking your head yes or no. Once you get a solid response that you know is correct you are ready to try to communicate. Just like the rods the pendulum can locate energy by moving toward it. Again this may sound strange but I have seen a pendulum move at a 45 degree angle and stay there while a cold spot moved right past the investigators in the room.

The more you use these types of items the more in tune they will become with you and your energy. While these nontraditional tools should not be used without their scientific counterparts, it's still fun to mix it up. Depending on the location and the ghosts that are present you may get a better response if the equipment is simple and unassuming to interact with, as opposed to having lots of bells and whistles.

12. HOW TO TALK TO CLIENTS

Learning how to talk to clients is something that my group now has a lot of experience with but there was definitely a learning curve along the way. I figured this chapter might save you from "foot in the mouth syndrome" and help you see what an important part of the investigation the client is. The client is not just a home or business owner, they are a piece of the puzzle and a wealth of knowledge if you know what questions to ask.

Steve getting ready to investigate the Andover House in Andover, NY

The number one thing to be considerate of when talking with a client is to be respectful. You never want to try to tell a client they are wrong or that what they are experiencing is not real. Always remember that it's real to them or else you wouldn't be there to investigate. Validation is something that most clients will need so whether you debunk what they are experiencing or you bring them evidence, you're validating them one way or the other.

I'll give you an example of what not to do when a potential client approaches you for help. I touched on this incident earlier, but here are the details of what happened. PRONE is very skeptical of orbs and especially photos of orbs. We feel that most times these photos are dust, bugs or moisture. In order for us to classify something as an orb it has to have two criteria. The first is that it has to have movement and the second it that it has to be self-illuminating. We were at a fund raiser a few years back where we had a table and were talking to people about what we do and just networking with other people in the field.

While we were there, a woman came up to our table with a photo of what she thought were orbs in her house. She wanted our opinion about whether or not we thought these were legitimate. So she showed a few of us the photo and we all clearly thought this was a photo of dust.

Here's where it got sticky. Instead of validating this woman and saying something like" this is an interesting photo, can you tell me more about it?" the investigator instead said "This is dust". The woman immediately became defensive and started to debate this with the investigator since she clearly disagreed. This turned into a back and forth conversation that went on for about 10 minutes before the woman took back her photo and left.

What kind of impression do you think she had of our group after that? Even if you know that you are right you should always be respectful when you are interacting with the public. First impressions are so important and you want to make the best one possible, especially because you may not get a second chance. It's a good idea to talk with your group about how to respond to questions from the public. Perhaps your group will want to appoint someone to speak on the group's behalf or maybe you just have a conversation about hot topics to ensure everyone is one the same page. It's much better to be over prepared then to stick your foot in your mouth.

When talking to a client you should always try to be understanding. Most of the time people don't have positive interactions with the paranormal and it's natural for people to be fearful of what they can't explain. Believe it or not, there is still a lot of stigma about ghosts and hauntings and it can be hard for people to come forward and especially to ask for help.

Whether it's a set of cultural beliefs or even religious ideals, sometimes people can be afraid to discuss what they have seen or felt. Your job as the professional is to help them feel comfortable to be able to open up about what's been happening in their home or business. Your main focus should be to set their minds at ease and to make sure they know they aren't alone. Having experiences with the paranormal can be very isolating for people and it's good to keep this in mind when talking to potential clients.

Sometimes it's easier for a client to write down what activity has been taking place in their home or business. We have two different ways that we have clients document what they are experiencing. The first thing we do is encourage the client to keep a journal of the activity taking place. We ask that they include the date, time and a brief description of what happened.

There are a few reasons for this, not only does this help us establish potential patterns but it also helps to have an accurate account of what took place. Often we remember things differently and the details fade over time. Looking for patterns may be a big help in figuring out what's going on. Residual hauntings will happen over and over again and sometimes having a client keep a journal can help show this since there may be days or weeks in between incidents.

If we are investigating a home we will ask more than one family member to do this to see if there is any correlation in what they have been experiencing. The other thing we do is have all the family members complete a form that asks very specific questions about the activity taking place. The form includes questions about when the activity first started happening, whether any notable events took place around the same time, where the activity usually happens and what exactly they've witnessed.

These forms become part of our case files and help us try to piece together why things may be taking place at this particular location. Clients usually find it much easier to write this information down than to talk about it openly.

While it's important to be respectful to a client and to reassure them, it's equally important to remain objective about what they tell you. You always want to think the best of people and that whatever they think is going on is legitimate to them, but don't be naïve. People lie... a lot. There are lots of reasons why people lie about activity. Some do it for attention or fame while others may do it for financial gain but whatever the reason it happens quite frequently. From time to time you will hear stories of people faking hauntings in their establishments.

Unfortunately the paranormal field has become corrupt in a lot of ways and this encourages people to lie about activity. It can save a business if it suddenly becomes haunted and has lots of activity, especially if the client charges a fee for groups to conduct investigations. While I understand the reasons most businesses charge fees, it doesn't hurt to ask what the fees go towards since most legitimate clients will be comfortable with telling you. Keep in mind that larger locations will charge more because their operating costs will be higher as well the maintenance required to keep the location open.

Make sure to use your gut when talking with and interviewing potential clients. If their claims seem beyond belief they usually are. I would suggest that you develop a form to use with each potential client prior to investigating. You will find that for the most part you get what you give. Treat the client how you want to be treated. Remember that they may be going through a rough and stressful time. Living with a haunting can wear a person down physically and emotionally and the client may be fragile by the time they reach out for help.

Alison Smith

13. HOW TO RUN INVESTIGATIONS

Conducting investigations are the most important thing you and your group will do. I wanted to share with you how PRONE runs investigations. You may find that some of this will work for your group or you may want to do things completely different from us. Whichever way you decide to go, make sure that you have some protocol in place. Not only can you present this to the client beforehand so they know what to expect but it will help guide investigators through the process as they learn their roles and it will give some order to the group as a whole.

After a potential client has made contact with PRONE (Paranormal Researchers of Niagara and Erie), the following protocol is put in place and outlines the procedures used in all of our investigations.

1. Our first contact will be made by phone or through email. An investigator will be asking you questions about your alleged paranormal activity and will be taking some quick notes. Please be as honest as possible with the investigator. After the initial conversation, an investigator will complete an initial report of your claim. This report will help our team determine if yours is a case we would be able to assist with.

   If upon initial contact; the investigator thinks you are not being honest or upfront with the required information, the investigator has the right to refuse service and the contact will end there. PRONE may decide that the case does not warrant immediate attention, or we also may refuse to conduct an investigation based on distance, cost or time.

Please also keep in mind that we are not trying to "prove" a haunting or the presence of an entity. We seek the truth about claims of paranormal activity. We only wish to research and investigate your claims and offer assistance in finding possible explanations for the activity that is being experienced.

2. After PRONE has received your claim by phone or email and we feel an investigation is warranted, we will send you a few forms to fill out to describe the activity in more detail. We may also ask you to start a daily journal to document the activity you are experiencing. Again, your honesty is pertinent for PRONE to complete a professional and thorough investigation. The more detail you can provide the better our investigation will be. After you have completed the forms, you will be required to return them in the enclosed self-addressed stamped envelope or through email.

3. After your forms have been returned and reviewed by PRONE, one of the investigators assigned to your case will contact you to schedule an onsite interview. During this interview one or more investigators will

meet directly with you to discuss your claims. We will review your forms; we may conduct interviews with any witnesses that have experienced the activity. These interviews are key for PRONE to complete the preliminary investigation.

4. During the onsite visit PRONE will also complete a walkthrough of the location of the activity. For the physical plant component of the investigation we will take notes, we may sketch diagrams, take photos and take readings of the environment with various types of equipment. If PRONE feels a full investigation is warranted, an investigator will schedule this with your consent. An investigation can be discontinued at any time if you no longer want our help.

5. When PRONE returns to complete a full investigation this is what you can expect:

- There will be anywhere from 2-6 investigations collecting data and conducting research. (There may be more investigations on site if PRONE finds this necessary)

- There will always be at least one Lead Investigator heading the investigation of your site. Our investigators never work alone.

- Expect the investigators to be there for several hours. They will need to go through all the areas included in the claims of paranormal activity. This may include but is not limited to the general areas where the activity has occurred, such as basements, attics, bedrooms, closets and the surrounding property.

- You may prohibit access to any area of the site in question, but please note that this may alter or even hinder our ability to conduct a thorough investigation. As a result, PRONE may determine the investigation to be inconclusive.

- We will be using all types of equipment including but not limited to recording devices, flashlights, cameras, walkie talkies, etc. We may need to tape down equipment or secure it for safety purposes.

- You can be present for the investigation, but we ask that you refrain from interfering with the investigation. This will allow us to have the least amount of distraction and/or tainted evidence. We ask that you either ask all your questions before or at the end of the investigation, please try to refrain from asking questions during sessions. Please always remember you can terminate an investigation at any time.

- Please expect that we will be making some amount of noise during the investigation. We may use devices that alarm, or equipment that flashes and may make small amounts of noise.

- Investigators may need to move quickly through the environment to retrieve potential evidence, so the areas should be free of debris and obstacles as much as possible.

6. After PRONE has completed a full investigation on site, we may complete some additional off site research by contacting past owners, going to the local library, historical society, village/town hall, etc. Lastly, PRONE will review all of the collected documentation and evidence gathered during your investigation and we will complete a thorough report

based on the evidence collected. PRONE will contact you to have the findings of the investigation presented in a timely manner.

7. At this time, PRONE will meet with you directly to show you any evidence recovered to support the findings of the investigation. This can include but not be limited to personal experiences, photos or visual images, audio sounds or recordings. This evidence is considered the property of PRONE; we can publish our findings on our website either publicly or anonymously based on the written consent from you, the client. We will allow you to determine which you would prefer. If requested we will also provide you with copies of any evidence we recover.

8. After the investigation has been concluded, PRONE may ask you to complete a referral letter based on your experiences with our group. This is completely voluntary, but we would appreciate your feedback on the investigation.

So there you have it, our protocol is pretty straight forward and it has been a work in progress. As I said before you should establish some sort of protocol, especially if you want to appear professional to the client and establishing a routine will help your investigations run much smoother.

We post our protocol right on our website for potential clients to view prior to contacting us. I've found it to be very helpful in that it sets the tone for our group from the start. Many clients have also remarked that they like that it was accessible to them beforehand.

14. TO PROVOKE OR NOT TO PROVOKE

Provoking in the paranormal world is probably one of the most serious issues that ghost hunters deal with. Whether or not you and your group do this or don't, be prepared to draw a line in the sand because how you feel about this is probably more emotional than scientific. In order to decide how you feel about this issue, I would suggest that you follow your gut. Either you will see or hear a fellow investigator doing this and it will make you very uncomfortable or you won't see what the big deal is and you will jump right in.

In order for you to understand why I feel the way I do about this issue, I wanted to share with you the first time I ever saw an investigator engage in this behavior and how it made me feel. First off I've never been a big fan of watching ghost hunting shows, especially after I started doing this work myself. I didn't have an opinion one way or the other on the issue of provoking because I thought that when people did it, it was to boost ratings and make their shows more interesting, I didn't think anyone actually went into a person's home or business and acted like this, but I was really wrong about that.

I was out with a few members of my group on a public investigation a few years back. We were at a well-known haunted located and the night had been going pretty well. Public investigations are always difficult due to the amount of people that attend and because the level of experience is so vast between participants, but everyone seemed to be getting along and some even claimed to have had some activity.

We were in a group of about 8 people, there was close to 30 people total and we were headed out to investigate a location on the grounds. The history of this location is known for the most part but there are still a few unanswered questions and I think the investigator in question was trying to get some concrete answers this particular night.

We were all standing around, with various kinds of equipment set up around the area and people began asking questions, trying to gets some kind of interaction going. Things were quiet and we weren't having much luck so this particular investigator stepped up and started asking some questions. At first this seemed like any other line of questioning but during this session things started to change. This investigator, for whatever reason, seemed to be agitated that there wasn't enough activity happening and the line of questioning completely changed. It went from being inquisitive to challenging and immediately started to make me uncomfortable.

The conversation became less about trying to communicate and more about showing off. This investigator was making comments about how "we aren't afraid or you", "come out and show yourself or are you to weak" and "your just a piece of crap". The atmosphere in the room started to change and I no longer wanted anything to do what was going on. To me, this no longer felt like investigating, it felt like bullying.

As I started to pick up my equipment to leave, the investigator started to suffer from a burning sensation on their arm which stopped the session. I'm not sure what caused the injury to this investigator but I also didn't want to stick around to find out. I packed up my stuff and left the investigation early and haven't done a public investigation with this group since.

So what exactly is provoking and why do people do it? Provoking in the paranormal field is quite literally trying to get a rise out of a spirit or trying to force a response by any means necessary. It is challenging a spirit to make a move or to engage them in confrontation. The easiest way I can explain it, is that it's like bulling someone into doing what you want. I have seen a few other people do this since that first experience I had and never once have I seen it lead to any kind of a positive outcome.

In my experience, when groups are trying to make a name for themselves, you tend to see that they engage in this type of investigating on a regular basis. Whether they are trying to create an image of being a tough no nonsense group or have hopes of one day making it big, it seems to be an acceptable technique that they see no problem with using, even if that means getting hurt. I have never known anyone to be scratched, hurt or hit unless they or someone in their group was provoking.

A member of my group (Kathy) occasionally helps out as a tour guide for a local museum on their overnight ghost hunts. One night she was working with a group who were having a slow night so they started to provoke in hopes of getting some reaction. Kathy tried to explain to the group that nothing good ever comes out of provoking and that the spirits at this particular location don't like it.

The group kind of laughed it off and didn't take her warning seriously at all and headed to the basement of this location. Once there they continued to provoke until one of the people in the group yelled out and ran upstairs. Once there the person was saying that they felt as if something had scratched their back and sure enough, upon inspection this person had a long red scratch down their back. Needless to say that ended their night since they were all afraid to continue after that.

So why doesn't PRONE provoke on investigations? Throughout the years of investigating, I've never had to resort to this as a way to boost activity. And besides, I don't know about you but I'd prefer to leave an investigation in the same condition

I started it in. Well besides the risk of bodily harm, to us it's just not right. We believe in respecting spirits and treating them the same as if they were alive. Don't they deserve that? Without knowing exactly why someone is still hanging around a location, it's very presumptuous of us to think we'll figure it out if we push.

Furthermore, last time I checked, we don't ever know who we are actually talking too! It could be Aunt Bess that you're calling a piece of crap because she keeps moving things around the house. It could be the spirit of a grieving parent, someone whose life came to a tragic end or a child who passed way too young. It seems irresponsible to me to act as if you know what's going on when you really have no clue.

Another reason why we don't provoke has to do strictly with residential hauntings. As I've said previously, we as investigators get to leave a location but the people who live in the house have to stay and deal with the aftermath. If you go into an investigation with guns blazing, yelling, cursing and demanding that whatever is there communicates with you, what do think will happen when you leave? You've left a nasty hostile bit of energy behind and did nothing to help anyone. Perhaps you've even made the situation worse for your own selfish gain.

It's no wonder that clients are leery about having people they don't know come into their homes. I can't tell you how many times people have told me about activity in the house but say they don't want it investigated because they are afraid whatever is going on will increase. Largely this is due to what little experience they have with the process of investigating and provoking is common place on lots of the shows they watch.

If you decide that you are going to put provoking in your arsenal for investigations, my only advice would be to be prepared for whatever happens. If you're in a bar and make fun of the guy sitting next to you and he turns around and punches you, whose fault is that? You have to be ready to deal with the consequences of your actions. If you don't want to be called dirty names during an EVP session then don't set the tone that way.

It's fair to mention that you may be provoked by spirit during an investigation too. If you turn on a Hack Shack and it immediately starts calling you names or saying threatening things, I would turn it off and walk away. Not only will you look silly arguing with a piece of equipment but trying to get any information out of that interaction will be a waste of time. Remember that personalities don't cease to exist when someone passes. But you as the investigator are in charge; you can set the tone for how the investigation will go. If you are hostile expect that to be reflected back at you. My biggest hope in writing about this topic is that people will realize that most groups don't engage in this type of interaction and if you are looking to join a group, you should ask about this before you are made to be uncomfortable or unsafe at someone's expense.

15. REVIEWING THE EVIDENCE

If you plan to run a group it's a good idea to have a set way to go through and review your evidence. Some groups may prefer to review evidence as a team others may do it independently but if you have some criteria it will make it easier for everyone and will make it more consistent in putting everything together for your client. If you plan to find a group to join, ask them how they review their evidence and what criteria they use. Depending on their answers you may know right away if this is a group you want to join or if you need to keep looking.

Alison Smith

In our group, we review our evidence independently but we share everything. What I mean by this is that no one would show a client a piece of evidence unless the group agrees that it is what it is. There are some rules we have for doing this and we stick to them. I trust that the way I review my evidence is the same way everyone in my group does it also. We decided to review evidence independently because it cuts down on the time it takes and if everyone can go at their own pace on their own time people won't rush to get through it. Going over evidence all together for hours at a time can be very draining, it's much more manageable if you can break it down into smaller review sessions as you have time.

Each member of my group can review their evidence whenever they want as long as it's turned in to be shared within a reasonable time. This is usually about a week post investigation. It's important to keep up with reviewing evidence so that you can get back to the client in a timely fashion, but also so you don't get backed up with what you have to go over. For every hour you record you will need at least that much time to review it.

This again is why you should be conscious of what your fellow investigators are doing. Take turns recording sessions and leaving recorders in different places. It's important to cover as much area as you can but it's difficult to face an evidence review of a quiet room for 6 hours too.

There are lots of programs you can get to review your evidence but if you're just starting out, I would suggest getting a free program like Audacity. The more expensive the program, the harder it is to use and evidence review is already a very tedious process. Audacity can be easily downloaded to your computer in a short amount of time and is ready for use as soon as the download is complete. If you want more information on how exactly this program works and how it's used specifically for ghost hunting consider reading" *Modern Technology and Paranormal Research"* by Rob Gallitto.

Once everyone has gone through their evidence it gets emailed to myself and PRONE's Tech Manager Rob, since we usually do the reveals for the client. We will review what everyone has sent and if anything is questionable we will send it out to the rest of the group for input. If it's an EVP we won't tell anyone what we think it says to see if others come up with the same explanation.

The reason for this is that if you already know what the EVP is supposed to mean you will be predisposed to hearing that. It becomes less about hearing what's actually there and your brain trying to match up the sounds you are hearing to what your brain thinks the voice should be saying. This is a trick used by paranormal shows all the time.

Think about it, how many times have you been watching a show and the investigator says we got an EVP and they play it on the air and you can't make out what if anything is being said. Then they play it again and say the EVP says "help me" suddenly you hear it again and yes that's what it says! How did you miss that the first time? It seems so clear now that you know what is says. We do this with clients too. When we play a clip for them we will play it a few times without telling them what we think it says. We don't want to taint what they hear and to me it lends even more creditability if they can hear the same thing we did.

As a group if we can't agree on a piece of evidence we throw it away. Unless everyone is on the same page there's no sense in moving forward with it. It's important that each member feels confident to stand behind whatever we think we caught, especially because we do a lot of public reveals and there's always someone in the crowd who wants to tear the evidence apart. This is one reason why we have a set way that we review evidence and we make this known to the public before we show them anything.

The rules are simple, we don't change the recordings we get in any way and we must all agree that it is what it is. However that EVP sounds on the recorder is how you will hear it through the program we use. We don't speed it up or slow it down. We don't filter it in any way. You will find that lots of the recording programs have all sorts of bells and whistles. And while these are fun to experiment with they are terrible for the credibility of EVPs. If you mess around with the speed and amplification of an EVP or even someone just saying something you can get it to sound like a demon from Hell asking just about anything.

This may sound like I'm being overly dramatic but unfortunately I've seen groups do just that. I was at an event where a lot of members of different groups were sharing evidence and this one group started telling everyone about a recent investigation they did at a residence. The people living there had been experiencing some unpleasant feelings in the home and felt there might be a negative presence there. The team went in and investigated and came back with a few EVPs.

The first thing they did was tell everyone what they thought they said before they even played them. This automatically taints the evidence but we tried to be opened minded anyway. As soon as the investigator played the EVPS clips, it was clear that they had been manipulated. The voice appeared male but was clearly slowed down and filtered to the point that it sounded inhuman. Now is it possible to get an EVP that actually sounds that way? Sure I think anything is possible but in the years I've been doing this I've never caught one.

The one good thing I can say about this group is that when someone asked if the EVP's had been manipulated they did admit to filtering them to make them clearer, but that blows the credibility for me right there. A good rule to work by is that if you have to alter something to make it easier to hear or see then chances are there wasn't anything there in the first place.

This is also why we try to take more than one photo at a time. You always want to have an establishing shot of any given area so you can go back and compare other photos to it. The same is said for video. Using the techniques we talked about early in this book such as tagging EVPs and writing down impressions of given areas will make your evidence review much easier as well as make it more credible to the client and the public.

It's sad to say that I always have to be highly skeptical of evidence captured by other teams just because there are no set standards for conducting evidence review. You just can't be sure someone hasn't manipulated their evidence in some one. With all the potential fame that can come from an amazing piece of evidence, the desire to fake things and manipulate them is high.

On the other hand, finding out that a group has faked something can ruin your credibility indefinitely. If you have hopes of doing this work for any period of time, I would follow your mom's sage advice. Honesty is always the best policy. I'd much rather admit that I didn't catch anything on an investigation than fake a piece of evidence just to say I did.

Alison Smith

**Cheryl heading in to investigate the Hinsdale House,
Hinsdale, NY**

16. PARANORMAL UNITY

If you are considering starting your own group, I want you to think about this idea of paranormal unity. You will see that for the most part it's not common practice for groups to work together and share information. About a year or two into being a paranormal investigator, I started hearing the buzz words "paranormal unity" and I immediately thought that this sounded like a great concept. Why not all work together for the greater good? But then reality set in and I began to see that this was not an idea that could thrive because of one single issue...Ego.

I've never understood why some groups stake claim to haunted locations and won't allow others the opportunity to investigate them as well. If you haven't experienced this yet, you will at some point and it's just plain sad. I will never understand why we can't actually work together and share information and knowledge as a group truly united under one banner. After all there are no real experts in a field that has no set standards of operation. We are all working in a field based entirely on theory. How can one of us be more right than the other?

So is this idea of paranormal unity really possible? If we, as investigators and researchers could put aside the desire to one up each other it might actually be. There is so much infighting and back stabbing that takes place on a daily basis, we have to try to get back to the foundations of why we started doing this work in the first place. We should all be here to learn and grow as people and to answer those questions we've been pondering for what seems like forever.

The Author, Steve and Tom while investigating the USS Sullivan in Buffalo, NY

I have always run my group in a manner that allows for the opportunity to work with others. We have been open with locations, connections and opportunities. This has always been important to me especially because of the hard time I had first breaking into the field. The only time I've ever held back information has been at the request of a client. We often investigate larger locations that require more manpower than we have. I've always called in people to come in and give us a hand not expecting anything in return and this has burned us a few times. It's hurtful when a fellow investigator uses your kindness as a means to get their own group into a location in the hopes of locking it down. Why can't we all just get along?

It also makes it difficult to promote this idea of paranormal unity with the current media influence. A year or so ago a show came on the air whose sole purpose it was to pit team against team in a weekly challenge. The whole idea was to see who could conduct a better investigation. The show ended each week with a winner and a loser. How can you really judge which team is better when it's all based on evidence gathered during an investigation? Last time I checked, spirits didn't perform on command or for TV cameras.

There was also a short lived show about an investigative team that took an unorthodox approach to investigating, so much so that they actually did a bloodletting ceremony on the air to try to ramp up activity. Do we really want the general public thinking that if they let us into their homes we'll be doing things like that? Really helps public relations, doesn't it?

There again comes the problem of the lack of standards. If we have no concept of what behavior is acceptable during investigations, we have to be understanding when people don't want their homes or businesses investigated. As we discussed in the previous chapter, we don't even review evidence in a uniform way. Most every team I deal with looks at evidence differently and then reviews it in their own way. What one group may think is a class A EVP may be ruled out or debunked by another.

These types of issues only help perpetuate the problems. It makes it hard to stand behind someone else's evidence when you have no idea how it was captured and discovered. Don't misunderstand me; as I've said before I'm not suggesting that there be only one way of doing things, but an acceptable standard can and should be established.

So where do we go from here? Should we wait around for other groups to fade out as they discover how much work this really is? Do you think the illusion of what we see in a 30 minute TV show has become the reality of watching and scrutinizing 18 hours of DVR footage for bugs and dust? Should we refuse to socialize with anyone who doesn't agree with the way we do things? Perhaps we should continue to let Ego influence our every move in the field? Of course not, if we really want true paranormal unity we need to start acting like a group of people devoted to a common cause. We need to start recognizing when we may need help from time to time and then be humble enough to ask for it with the realization that there just may be someone who knows more than you do. It's ok to not have all the answers and to not know how to deal with every situation. That's why unity is so important. It gives you a pool of people to draw on when you need that help.

We have to be supportive of each other in trying new techniques and ideas for the purpose of furthering the field. What a new concept! How great would it be if we could try building each other up instead of tearing each other down. As a group we don't post evidence on our website because we have seen so much infighting about what other groups think is or isn't credible.

I'm not suggesting that everyone needs to be best friends and sit around a camp fire holding hands and singing songs, but we do need to have a mutual respect for each other as colleagues. After all, mutual respect is the very foundation of paranormal unity and something that is severely lacking in our current state.

I used to think that this was a local problem associated with where my group is from since there are so many paranormal groups in a small area, but in traveling around and interacting with many different paranormal groups I see the same problems in lots of places. This is not an isolated problem; it's an epidemic in the field. Because this field is so open and since anyone can start a group there is an abundance of groups with no guidance and no idea where to turn for help or direction.

We, as paranormal investigators have a responsibility to ourselves and to each other to make all the hard work we do be worth something. We are living in a time where technology is giving us insight into the paranormal on levels we never thought possible. We are making discoveries and finding new evidence on a daily basis. If we can't find a way to work together and to come to a common consensus about what we are doing, how can we ever hope to enlighten our peers and face the skeptics? They don't need to tear apart our evidence. We do that to each other constantly, very methodically without any outside help.

But fear not, all hope is not lost. If we all decide to unfriend our friend Ego, we may have a chance to turn this around. If you are starting your own group, don't let yourself be jaded by this chapter. Come into this knowing the challenges we are all facing so you can be part of the solution.

We have enough people who want to look down their noses at everyone else, be open minded about working together and share what you know. As paranormal investigators we need to ask ourselves one question: Is it more important to be right or is it more important to be willing to listen? I myself have my ears wide open.

Members of PRONE hanging with Zombies at the Parahorror Convention at the Buffalo Central Terminal, Buffalo, NY

17. TIPS ON HOW TO BOOK INVESTIGATIONS

One of the questions I always get from people just starting out in the paranormal field is, "How do I get started finding places to investigate?" Depending on how many paranormal teams are already located in your area, this may be easier or more difficult than it was for me. I was naïve in the beginning and just thought that I could contact places that I knew had hosted investigators in the past and just ask to book an investigation. I found out quickly that there were a lot of politics involved that I had no idea existed. The hardest part in booking investigations is finding the locations. Since we started we have been able to investigate some amazing places and perhaps these tips will help you do the same.

One of the many long halls in the stacks at the Buffalo and Erie County Public Library

The first tip in trying to book investigations is research, research and more research. This is the best way to find out about locations that probably haven't been investigated yet, but have a haunted history. In finding a brand new location you won't have to deal with the impressions other groups may have left with the owners and you will have the opportunity to be the first team to document activity, if there is any.

The down side of a brand new location can be trying to convince whoever owns the property that they should let you investigate. There are a few things you can do to increase the likelihood of this happening and we will discuss them in the next few pages.

Researching can be difficult if you don't know where to start so the internet can be a great source. Lots of people have posted all kinds of information about places that are known to be haunted. Another place to check out is the local historical society, just be cautious that people may not want to talk about the paranormal. Not everyone believes in the same things we do, so be sensitive to that when inquiring about local history.

You might also want to check out your local bookstore since most places have at least one book based on its haunted history. If you're in the western NY area, *"Ghosts of Buffalo"* by Tim Shaw is a great book to check out.

Another good way to do your research is to get out there and meet other groups. Networking is a huge part of the paranormal community. Although there may be some places that groups will keep close, there is usually a few that they are willing to share. The best advice I can give in talking to other groups is to offer something in return. If a group gives you a lead on a potential investigation, share something you know or offer to take a few of their group members the next time. One hand does wash the other and sharing is a good step towards paranormal unity.

If you are looking to meet other groups and network I would suggest getting involved in a few of the paranormal conventions. There is usually one taking place every few months and they are a great way to start to meet others and put yourself out there. We usually do a few of these a year and have met some great people as a result. Not only do you get to see what other equipment or techniques people are using you can also get an inside track about which are the best locations to go investigate and which ones you can skip.

It would also be a good idea to see if there is a meet up of some sort in your area and if there isn't, it may be something you want to start. Meet ups are usually a monthly meeting where a group of likeminded people get together for the purpose of networking. There are a few of these meet ups that relate to the paranormal already in my area and I have attended most of them for different periods of time.

Although meet ups are great when you are first getting started, most of the time you will outgrow it on some level. The problem is that the meet ups are always welcoming new people, and although this is great, it makes it difficult for the veterans to learn and continue to grow. If you find this to be the case, consider starting a group yourself. I co-founded a group called TRS (The Research Society) which meets monthly and is geared towards experienced investigators.

Each moth there is a topic for discussion and everyone does research and brings what they have learned to share with the group. This has really helped us continue to grow and we continue to have great discussions. Everyone helps to decide what the topics will be and nothing is off the table. It has allowed us to examine other paranormal topics like cryptozoology, that most typical meet ups don't have the opportunity to research.

When you are trying to locate potential investigation sites don't forget about the easiest resource to tap into… your friends and family of course!. We have had a lot of our leads come from someone who knows someone who knows someone. Getting the word out to your family and friends usually works well since they will probably be more accepting of what you are trying to do and will keep their eyes and ears open to any opportunities that may pop up. I think we have made more connections that have panned out this way than any of the other ways we use. Besides your family and friends won't want anything in return expect maybe to go along with you.

So what do you do when you finally have a few places to contract to try to book investigations? Most locations that offer public and/or private hunts will usually have a set fee for either a group or per investigator. Whether or not you think the fee is reasonable is up to you. It doesn't hurt to ask what the fee goes towards if you feel the amount is questionable. Keep in mind that the larger the building the larger the fee will usually be.

If you are trying to book a location that doesn't usually allow investigations, offering to pay a fee or make a donation is a great way to get your foot in the door. Sometimes the only thing holding an owner back is paying for a staff to be there overnight or keeping the heat on. Offering to make a donation or pay a fee also shows that you're serious.

If you are trying to book a public location that won't take a donation for whatever reason, you can offer to do a reveal of the evidence for the public. This has also worked well for us. We usually give some sort of lecture and then show the evidence and this brings people into the location that might not otherwise stop in.

If you feel that the owner of a location is on the fence there are a few more things that may help you seal the deal. You can always share your protocol with them and talk to them about their specific concerns. If you can answer questions confidently, it will help the owner feel more comfortable with you and your group. You may also want to provide them with a few references.

Try to make sure the references you are giving them are from places that are similar. For example, if you are trying to book an investigation at a private residence, don't give them references for large well known locations. You should be trying to set their mind at ease so give them references of people they can talk to and that they can relate to.

The last thing you should consider is giving them a copy of your confidentiality clause. Having the public know a business is haunted is not always a great thing depending on what kind of business it is. A home owner may also not want their neighbors to know that they are experiencing some kind of activity that they can't explain.

If you can put their minds at ease by ensuring confidentiality, it may be the last push someone needs to allow the investigation to take place. It would be great if everyone was on board right away and sought you out, and lots will, but there will always be those few that may take some convincing. If you take the time in the beginning to work with the owner to feel better about the investigation it will pay off in the end.

18. REALITIES OF THE PARANORMAL

We have touched on some of the realitics of ghost hunting a few times in other parts of this book, but I wanted to take the time to really discuss what ghost hunting is actually like. Doing this even on a part-time basis will take a personal commitment and you should know what you're in for. Ghost hunting is not glamorous, yes you heard right, it's not jam packed with activity and doesn't fit neatly into a 30 minute program. These realities are not meant to discourage you but just to inform you, so you will be better prepared when you begin your quest.

I wanted to write this chapter because most people don't see any other side to investigating besides what they are exposed to through the media. If that's what it was like all the time, we would be light years ahead of where we are in gathering evidence and there would be even more people doing this than there currently is.

I wanted to take the time to make sure you truly understand the amount of work that goes into running a paranormal group. If you've decided by this point that you are going to find a group to join, still read through this so that you will have an idea of what the person in charge of that group goes through. It will at least give you some insight into why they get mad when things don't go how they should. Maybe you'll be a little more understanding having read this.

For me this chapter is almost like being in a confessional. Talking about the ins and outs of running a group is probably not something most founders want to discuss because we have to keep up the pretense of having everything run smoothly and be perfect. But like most things when you get into doing them, you'll find there is a good amount of work that you will need to do in order to be and to stay successful.

Running a paranormal group takes a lot of patience and even more persistence. Not only is everyone looking to you to keep things moving forward, but you are always expected to on top of your game. Making contacts, booking investigations, coordinating the schedule, the list of responsibilities is lengthy. Even if you do a great job at delegating things to other members of your group, you are still left holding the bag if something doesn't happen as it should. Everyone will get to pick and choose which investigations they can and want to do, you will be expected to be at very one.

You will schedule, conduct and execute group business and often raise issues and deal with conflicts that everyone else gets to avoid. It's a difficult job, but I won't have it any other way. I've been lucky to find the best people in the field to be members of PRONE and as much hard work as it's been, and will always be, it's worth it. When I say that investigating is not glamorous, I mean that for the most part the public only sees the best parts of what takes place. They don't see the Johnny on the spot since the location has no indoor plumbing or the space heaters because there is no heat. They don't see the "presents" left by mice, stray cats, raccoons, pigeons, bats and other animals that may have taken up residence in the location. They don't see the dust you breathe in and the debris you wade through to move from one area to the next.

Since many of these locations have been abandoned or shut down for decades, (think hospitals, asylums, schools) most places are in some sort of disrepair. There are a few places I've investigated that were in such bad shape that I ended up coming straight home and jumping into the shower. Yup I can honestly tell you that I've been more afraid of bats and rats than of ghosts in at least a few locations.

I was on an investigation of a well-known location in Ohio and no one mentioned to us that there were bats in the building, this happens more often than not. As we were making our way to an area of the building we stopped to run an EVP session. We set everything up and started to ask some questions when suddenly something came swooping through the room and all of us crouched down to avoid whatever it was.

After a few seconds we realized it was definitely a bat and started to back out of the area only to be bombarded by about ten more friends of our bat buddy. Just picture about 5 investigators trying to get out of one very small doorway while being dive bombed by a large group of hungry bats. Needless to say we took a lot more caution moving around this location after that. It just goes to show that you never know exactly what you'll find and you have to be hyper aware while investigating.

If I haven't mentioned it enough already the expense of ghost hunting is a very real thing. You may think that just the start up would be the main expense and once you get the equipment then you should be all set for the most part, but the startup expense is just the beginning. Equipment is always evolving and not to mention breaking and needing to replaced. As you grow and gain more experience, you will want new and better equipment to meet your needs. Even though I mentioned earlier on that you don't need to spend a lot to get started, equipment will be on ongoing expense.

Another expense will be the actual cost of investigating. If you try to go to the same places you see on TV you will find that it will make you broke. Large well know haunted locations can cost upwards of a thousand dollars a night if you want a private hunt. Not included in this price is also the travel costs themselves. Admission, food, lodging, gas, tolls the list goes on and on and most people don't think about that when they book a cool location 8 hours away.

Spending time away from your loved ones is also a serious reality of ghost hunting. I have seen quite a few relationships fall apart because one person was into ghost hunting and the other wasn't. For myself, I have to say that this has not been a factor in my personal relationships. My husband has always been supportive of me in everything I do, but the same can't be said for friends of mine. The key to working this out is being able to strike a balance.

Finding a balance is a good idea not only so that you don't lose touch with the world around you, it's also good so you get a break. Spending a lot of time in locations with tragic histories and possible bad energy is not a good thing for anyone.

Ghost hunting can also be a bit addictive. Once you get a taste for what can be seen and heard you want to see what else is out there. For most people this isn't a problem, but if you find yourself investigating every weekend, traveling and becoming out of touch with the people in your life who are still alive, this may be a problem. Too much of a good thing can turn bad quickly. Trying to contact dead people should never be a bigger priority than connecting with the actual people around you.

Alison Smith

Full Spectrum shot of the Lackawanna Library, one of our favorite places to investigate.

19. WHERE ARE WE HEADED?

What's next for the Paranormal Field...

Looking back over the years, it's unbelievable to see the strides the paranormal field has made. Not only are we more main stream now than we have ever been, we are in a technological age that continues to advance along with the investigators. So what can we expect from the future and what responsibilities do we have moving forward if any?

Paranormal Unity is an idea that has to take root in order for us to thrive. We need to put aside differences and find our commonality to work together to bring the experiences we share into the general public. In order for ghost hunting and paranormal research to be taken seriously we have to share what we know and what we've discovered without fear of ridicule and jealously from each other.

If you decide to start your own group, have a direction. Make sure your group has a common philosophy and make teaching and sharing a part of everything you do. Get educated on the paranormal, do your research and help others along the way. I really wanted to put this book together to help groups get started and if they are already established, then to be stronger.

We have to demand standards of practice of ourselves and our peers. How can we expect others to take us seriously if we can't even agree on the basics? Be consistent in the way that you conduct your investigations and review your evidence. Be a role model to other investigators and teach them the ropes, don't ignore them and dismiss them.

Try to stay on the cutting edge of the up and coming technology available to our field. Consider starting a research society of your own and invite others to join so you can learn as a community. Be open to other ideas and ways of doing things.

There will always be a new TV show or a new para-celebrity to follow, but keep in mind that for the most part, these are fads that will disappear as quickly as they come. Don't let the public ideal be what they see on TV.

The reality is that we are living in exciting times and we should take advantage of it. The veil between our world and that of the paranormal has never been thinner. Many people claim to have been touched in some way by the spirit world, more so than ever before. America as a nation is becoming more spiritual, not more religious. People are looking for outlets to talk about the paranormal and what they've experienced. You may be that connection.

No one can say for sure what the future of ghost hunting will look like. With the advancements of cameras and recording devices we can only assume that the evidence will get better and better. Wouldn't it be something if that grainy image of a shadow could be refined to show a man standing there? We may finally be able to answer some of those questions we've all been pondering since we started doing this work. If you think this sounds farfetched, just look at some of the evidence from 10 or 20 years ago. We've already come so far.

To know where you are headed you have to figure out what kind of ghost hunter you are. Hopefully by this point you have some idea, you should know whether or not you want to start a group or if you want to join on. You should have some feeling about a few of the controversial topics we are facing today. If you're reading this last chapter, I know you aren't in it just for the scare factor. I could have written a book just about all the crazy experiences I've had investigating and I thought about it, but at the end of the day I felt this content was more important.

If this book helps one group become established, I'll feel that the many hours at my laptop were well spent. There will be plenty of time to write about all the cool things I've seen and the evidence I've caught. Right now it's too important to not try to reach out and help people who want to ghost hunt in a responsible manner.

As I have said so many times before, take what's in here and make it your own. Try things out and see what works for you. This book is merely a guide and meant to give structure and direction to those who want it. I didn't invent any techniques discussed and can't take credit for creating anything brand new. Just as you have learned from us, we have learned from others. The last bit of advice I want to leave you with is this.. Surround yourself with good people. It will be hard to find the perfect people to be members of your group, I got lucky. I can truly say that PRONE is my family.

I could not do what I do without them and just like a family, we may have disagreements and not always get along perfectly, but we are always loyal to each other. In this ever changing paranormal world, it's priceless to know that there are a few people who will always have your back and will follow you into dark dank places without question.

So all that is left to say is get out there and investigate! Happy Hauntings!

FOR FURTHER READING

Spiritual Crossover is a book that discusses the relationship between the Metaphysical and the Paranormal. It's written by Medium Glenn White and Paranormal Investigator Alison Smith and chronicles some of their favorite investigations.

Copies are available at www.paratechstore.com

FOR FURTHER READING

Modern Technology and Paranormal Research is a detailed look at everything tech in the paranormal field. Written by Rob Gallitto, it's a wealth of information for anyone just starting out to the experienced investigator and shouldn't be missed.

Copies are available at www.paratechstore.com

Alison Smith

A NOTE FROM THE AUTHOR

Thank you for talking the time to read this book. If you have any questions related to the topics discussed, please feel free to contact me through PRONE's web site listed below or through our Facebook page.

www.pro-ne.org

www.facebook.com/prone.paranormal

Cover art work and design by:

Rob Gallitto

Made in the USA
Lexington, KY
04 February 2018